MW00991483

Similar titles by Belt Publishing

*A Detroit Anthology*

*How to Live in Detroit Without Being a Jackass*

# THE
## *Detroit*
# NEIGHBORHOOD
# GUIDEBOOK

**Edited by Aaron Foley**

First edition 2017

ISBN: 978-0-9989041-3-9

Belt Publishing
1667 E. 40th Street #1G1
Cleveland, Ohio 44120
www.beltmag.com

Cover and book design by Haley Suzanne Stone

# Contents

# Foreword

## *Aaron Foley*

No matter how many books are done about Detroit, it's still impossible to capture this city's ethos into a finite number of pages.

But damn if we don't come close sometimes. The vision for this guidebook was to showcase the many voices of this complicated city—as many as we possibly could. Those voices are shaped by the neighborhoods they know, or knew.

You can bond with someone in Detroit on three levels: what side of town they're from, what school they went to, and what neighborhood they're from, or, in many cases, what cross streets they lived near if the name of the neighborhood was never settled on. Our neighborhoods mold us. Whether you grew up in that neighborhood, bought your first house there, or had family there, it shapes you.

I remember many years ago, one of my cousins in Ypsilanti bragging about knowing some people over on Sussex Street in Detroit. Me having grown up there, I never knew Sussex to be, well, a big-name street—not on the level of, say, Schoolcraft, Joy Road, Houston-Whittier, or Dexter. But now I realize it was cool for him to actually know people in Detroit. I mean, nobody shouts out streets in Ypsilanti. But even a relatively innocuous street like Sussex could hold weight.

That's what this guidebook is all about. It's a dedication to all the streets, all the hoods, all the blocks, all the sides, and Hamtramck and Highland Park, too. Maybe every street isn't named, but if you are Detroit, you can recognize your story—your voice—in these entries.

We came close. Really close.

# Motor Nation

### Zoë Villegas

*I* was sixteen years old, just like most American teenagers, when I got my driver's license. But it was not that wholesome. And Detroit is not like the rest of America.

After weeks of practice in Elmwood Cemetery and months of driver's ed, my anxiety was working against my experience and making me a worse driver. But I had a lot of mercy from the teacher nicknamed Jazz Man, who would stoically sit in the passenger seat, encouraging me with, "Just relax, ya dig?"

Jazz Man was the most qualified to handle the stress of taking screaming teenagers on the road because—we suspected—he was under the influence. The only time I ever heard of him getting shaken up was by my own accomplishment. I landed the car in a ditch behind the train station with a group of girls who'd been driving since age twelve. For me, it was hopeless.

And then they announced that the funding ran out and we were told that driver's education would no longer be offered in Detroit Public Schools. I was granted my permit by default and sent on my way to take my road test.

In the early 2000s, the internet was not as prominent a source of information, so it was all word of mouth when it came to finding a place that I could trust to pass me. I was tipped off by someone that there was a guy who would do it for $75. The big day happened and I met this guy in a church parking lot where I proved to have made exactly zero progress since day one of driving, knocking over every cone. The test was really just for the sake of ceremony, and without even moving on to parallel parking, I got my license.

My mother had a van that she entrusted to my twin sister and me because it was on its way out. I now had a way to get six people to skip school at Western International High School with me and drive to the movie theater Downriver. Fairlane Town

Center was on lockdown and you could not sneak in it at all anymore. You would not be permitted in without an adult chaperone. This is what we had done all through the previous years, but now we had one less option of places to go. This was how I imagined the days of Stalin felt.

There was very little to do but drive around. Downtown was desolate at the time. We would drive down Michigan Avenue to the rich landscape of deep Southwest Detroit to Zug Island to Fort Wayne to peer at the most haunted-looking houses, drinking cups of Telway coffee to keep us awake. We would make the rounds to visit every friend that we knew working the various fast-food drive-in windows from Livernois to Chene. We would end our nights at a five-hour-long double feature at the Ford-Wyoming Drive-In, making it home at the break of dawn.

I worked for $8 an hour at the Campbell Branch library shelving books, and every cent I earned went into my gas tank because after we sold the van, I bought a 1989 Mercury Grand Marquis. The Grand Marquis, which I named the Betty Ford, cost about $70 to fill up and had to be refilled multiple times a week. The catalytic converter was stolen, the muffler dragged and was held up by a coat hanger, and there was some other problem that led the car to die frequently when idling. It was expensive to drive even though it was hardly luxurious. But driving was my pastime and everywhere I went, someone made an offer for that car, seeing in it exactly what I did: that it was Detroit Beautiful, meant for cruising. I had a close friend who was petite enough to hide in the trunk when we paid for our tickets, and we made this our regular ritual. I would pick up her and anyone else who wanted to come along—sometimes enough people to fog the car windows—and we would drive and drive and drive.

That summer, I was in the drive-thru line at Dairy Queen with a friend on a one-hundred-degree day. The car died and nearly caused a riot. Cars honked as we dripped sweat. A dozen people tried to jump it, diagnose it, or yelled for us to move. Two men pushed the back of the car into traffic on Michigan Avenue and followed us three miles home, going at a snail's pace. No air conditioner, windows unable to roll down. I finally had to sell the Betty Ford. A year later, the buyer returned, asking if I wanted to buy it back. I said no, but he also returned to me my blanket and pillow, which were left in the trunk by mistake—souvenirs of drive-in heists and cruisings past.

Ten years later, and the saga of finding a means of transportation continued. I really needed a car and I decided to go to a charity car auction. Here, the cars were donated for low-income people to bid on after going through the bureaucratic process of first proving you were poor, and then buying a yearly membership that allowed you to bid on cars once a month.

I woke up early for this spectacle. There was a long line, hot dog vendors, people directly outside the gates who had won a car at auction the day before and were selling it for a higher price across the street to people who didn't want to spend all day bidding. There were people complaining that they went with family members to bid on a car and when they got out of the auction, their family's car had been stolen and supposedly entered into auction later. This was what you called Motor City Purgatory.

The announcer, with a flair for the dramatic, got on a loudspeaker. "On your marks, get set, go!" he said, as the gates opened and a crowd gathered around a 1980s Buick with a broken windshield and no passenger door. A character in a Mad Max-like motorized contraption with Plexiglas around it and a foghorn attached barked out bids.

Bidding could take sometimes an hour; we moved on and on down the line between reasonably-taken-care-of, middle-of-the road cars, on to cars that looked like they must have been firebombed at that very spot because otherwise, there was no way they could have been transported there; on to scooters, jet skis, lawn mowers. They auctioned off anything with a motor.

Watching a crowd of one hundred move from car to car and seeing the last person realize that they were following a crowd over to a pair of jet skis was priceless. As it got silent, you could hear the last person pushing their way to the front: "ARE YOU SERIOUS, MAN?!"

As I was walking past the entrance at the charity car auction, I noticed another area with nicer cars. There was no doubt some racketeering going on that kept those cars in their own pearly gates. I saw a 1956 pink Cadillac, just like I'd always dreamed of owning, just like the one Elvis Presley bought his mother, Gladys. And then I was reminded of the Betty Ford. The gas it took, getting stuck at DQ, and knowing that no matter how beautiful this car was, that life is never that easy. To own that car, I would have to have a different life. And that life would most likely not include consuming this city's scenery like an optic form of sunbathing. I would be on the freeway, driving as fast as I could, not staring in awe at the mecca before me with the fear and respect of witnessing a twister.

Sometimes when I am driving down the freeway and see a billboard on the northwest side for the donated car auction, I think of the reasons I love Detroit, where we stand outside the gates of an auction just trying to find a way to get our hands on the same thing for which we built this city.

# Dispatch from SW Detroit:
## Seven Generations Seeking Good Home, Good Faith, Strong Will, Hard Working A.K.A. Get Your Own Damn Holiday and Stop Dressing Up Like a Fucking Mexican

*Michelle Martinez*

On the dawn of Cinco de Mayo, I brace for another rowdy celebration, droves of drunk settlers descending on my backyard, leaving urine, vomit, and trash in their wake. Cinco de Mayo, a holiday Mexicans and Mexican Americans rarely celebrate. But a holiday, nevertheless, to which this Latinx is forced to bear witness every year. Every year, I cringe at the sombreros and ponchos, the fake mustaches. I want to write an open letter to those who don them, about why this is akin to blackface, or Native American Halloween costumes. Perhaps we can work through the intellectualism of the violence of colonization, othering, and erasure, enter into dialogue about our bodies, and right to sovereignty. But this year, I reflect on this trauma over five generations in a four-block radius, collectively through time and space, and then through the witnessing of the changing in the land—this phase of colonization called gentrification. My family and this land are two clauses within the footnote of some history book, unseen or unwritten. This is a dispatch from Detroit's small Latinx diaspora, SW Detroit, Mexicantown, the US-Canadian border, frontera norteña, from my back window.

First, I want to talk what's what since the 1994 signing of NAFTA, the North American Free Trade Agreement. The land speculation in SW Detroit started then—for the bridge, for trade—but it was also the subsequent migration. Many people left Mexico because NAFTA hollowed out not only U.S. factories but also Mexican farms, thanks to huge U.S. agricultural subsidies. Farmers had to flee because they couldn't compete with Kraft cheese. I start there.

Dispatch, NAFTA: I'll tell you of the gang war between the Latin Counts and the Sur 13 which included tagging, shootouts, the burning of three houses, the home raid of an elder, and the portrait of two Red Berets standing in front of her house who couldn't prevent its eventual burning. I'll tell you about the eviction of a family because of a slumlord who didn't pay the taxes, and his tenant who had unpaid workdays but no recourse because his employers knew he didn't have papers. The eviction of this family resulted in the collapse of a budding friendship between two six-year old girls. I'll tell you about witnessing a woman watch a house be bulldozed by the forces of a millionaire magnate, the sole owner of the international bridge to Canada. She held a picture frame and cried in the alley as the house was smashed into the ground, leaving a vacant lot. And I'll tell you that was not the only house, and not the only woman.

I want to always remember the names of Maria and her children, I want to see their faces, now after returning to Mexico to be with their deported father, picked up on his way to work by ICE. Their two-year-old helped me plant the garden in the lot where the house was bulldozed. Where is the family now that was fixing their minivan to transport their four kids when the bank foreclosed on their home? I know where the hipsters who currently occupy it are, drinking $5 espresso that takes twenty minutes to slow brew. This is all just on my block. NAFTA made Detroit the busiest northern border crossing, broke apart so many homes, forced migration for labor—and with this came more policing, more security services, more trucks, more pollution.

In SW Detroit, you see many police: mounted police, rail police, Detroit Public Schools police, the Ambassador Bridge Security, the flashing lights of SWSOL, private security guards, border patrol, Homeland Security, Wayne County Police and State Police, and the Detroit Police Department.

Some residents participate in citizens' patrol, and cooperate openly with police. Yet crime and safety are almost like a caste system, separating those protected and those committed to prison. Unregistered landlords fined, garbage cans left on the curb, too. Unpaid taxes? Evicted. No money for water? Shut off. Police are chasing poor black and brown teenagers down the street, a drug bust to account for half-grams of medical marijuana, handing out a nine-count felony for graffiti while rape kits collect dust, while murder remains nightly news. This is the message: if you climb out of poverty, get out or go to jail.

Yes, some are happy with more police, happy that higher property values will get them more for their property. Maybe they can stop fearing home invasion, maybe they can finally move to the suburbs, retire somewhere warm, with dignity. Some can now finally afford their subprime mortgages on the rents of wealthy Brooklynites, a small stopgap in eviction. I wish all the assistance could've arrived sooner—fixed the roof under your tarp before you gave up, given out small grants to replace the melted siding from the fire, served you some help before giving up the business, battling depression, drug abuse, and abandonment, imprisonment. If only we could've defeated Clinton's NAFTA, would it have prevented the loss of your son to gang war, or the selling of the tortilla shop? Maybe then our schools wouldn't have closed, our language wouldn't have been stripped from the classroom.

Twenty-two years later, we see how NAFTA paved the path for gentrification. Those with access to capital are winning spaces and places that others simply cannot afford.

Dispatch, Gentrification: I want to show the world the photos of the family that lived in the neighboring historic home for generations, the furniture they put into a huge dumpster filled three times over. A tax eviction, it was then auctioned once at $30,000 while the living heir cared for his dying uncle. I want you to see the faces of the men who squat the green house, the fake injury one uses to lure more donations from Canadian tourists, and the guitar his comrade carries. He works as a security guard. I want to know what they will do when the new family moves in to the house purchased off the auction block from under a Chinese investor for half the price, $22,000, because they work for the city. And of course now, self-proclaimed "baby Gatsby" put a bar in the place of a community center, bought up two more houses with that good California money. The repeated murmurs of renaming Mexicantown, and the remapping of its boundaries to create a kinship with Corktown, West Corktown, or Millennial Village—this blank slate narrative.

For years, I loved the smell of fresh grass, but I know now that the cutting is the smell of gentrification, as the lawnmowers ride through the boulevards. Not all the city is cut, you see. For this, I find myself loving the night's darkness, because I know that for every LED street lamp turned on here, there is another turned off in another corner of the city, leaving it unofficially/officially "decommissioned." I want you to see the two sides of the mirror. It is as if we are playing Monopoly here with two unequal currencies, two sets of rules.

NAFTA and its subsequent export of jobs, gentrification, the buying up of property by the wealthy, white newcomers to recreate the neighborhood, are phases of colonization going back before 1701. The empty lots where my mother's mother's home stood were bulldozed by I-75 decades before globalization. The overpass freeway easement is the remains of my great-grandparents' home, and occasionally the military recruitment billboard pops up as its flag. They came here in 1915 because they were run off the southern border. We, Latinxs of SW Detroit, are the seventh generation, who began this struggle on the frontera Mexicana when the Treaty of Guadalupe Hidalgo was signed, who fled from forced relocation onto the reservations, who got kicked out of Mexico, who came north with a dream on the coattails of the Great Migration to the lands stolen from Anishnnabe. Are we now only fated to repeat the destiny once again on the frontera norteña? One hundred years later, we're still seeking a home, a land.

[The soundtrack to this dispatch from SW Detroit is barges and fire trucks, the hum of I-75, rancheros, and dubstep. The music competes on the bars of a single notation, yet only one is in diminuendo as quinceñeras, and bodas, disappear.]

The appropriation that happens every year on Cinco de Mayo, in the age of the

gentrification of Mexicantown, is added insult to injury—another phase of colonization, a word that—like capitalism, patriarchy, white supremacy—I have learned
to discuss the blunt object that forces brown and black people to hate ourselves so
much that we believe we don't deserve to exist. To be silent and be humble. To work
hard, and suffer to thrive. To pray in faith, but without hope. To endure and witness the dismantling of our identities, like at every Cinco de Mayo. Others have the
citizenship or the skin color to dress up in sombreros and ponchos, drink Coronas,
sing "Margaritaville," and get "white girl" smashed, and they are applauded, even
rewarded. Maybe they are not at risk of losing it all from dislocation, or deportation
like those who serve them in the restaurants where they eat. For me, it's a reflection
of Trump-style nationalism, awakened in the last election cycle, which thrives in the
culture of "New Detroit." It values money over memory, dispossession over democracy. And it's a mockery of the last thing we have the right to own—our own culture
and identities.

# What Wikipedia Won't Tell You about Delray, Michigan, 48209

### Scheherazade Washington Parrish

You can smell Delray
from three different cities.
In the summer, Delray smells like the shit that burns
and under the I-75, it rains exhaust all year.

The skies are streaked yellow during the day, and
someplace between steel and sewerage
the smell of pancakes, fish, and grits
wakes a household.

In the miasma of waste and Zug
a grandfather calls his granddaughter Shank
and teaches her to sow New Year's collards
in the front yard.

Someplace, between Yale and West End streets,
that grandfather's daughter remembered him
in beds of mustards, and tomatoes. She teaches
her daughter that onions are lilies.

Someplace between funk and rot, folks
are tired of not being able to breathe in the day
tired of not being able to sleep at night.
My father lives there, still.

Some nights, if you listen closely
you can hear the neighborhood hum
something between stench and haze
between song and secret.

# Cass Corridor #1

### *Joel Fluent Greene*

If I'm to talk about the corridor I know
The narrow, suffocating stroll
Where street walkers in neon clothes
Or threads
Would walk up Cass with tricky goals

The darkness of it all
Still
20 years later
The danger of parking on side streets lurking
The late night quests to visit mainstay buildings
With shiny new names
That reflect this new village
This commune of consumers
With expensive bicycles

I just want to be accepted!
Not as new
As authentic
Said the black man
Wit the jitney
Before the Uber
And the Lyft
He was part of the economy
Before this dichotomy
The halve called a nots
Another called the gots

I won't forget about the GOATS
I'll remember the names
The characters, the dark rooms
The deep base and sticky floors
For Sale signs slapped on a ghost

Ghosts that can't be revived
Only replaced
I'm familiar with the haunts
All the stories that took place

This corridor I know
Spin me round blindfolded
On some street off Cass
I'll find my way home
Or find my way to The Bronx Bar
Perhaps that's preferable
For the drowning of a sorrow
Thoughts of friends I used to know
When all of this shiny
Was fresh and exciting
Oh!
We would walk past the Bronx
The white and black faces
Now older, still nameless
Still way cooler than me

A punk song for crazy Dan
For East Palmer and Woodward
Regret that we never played chess
On your old glass countertop
Kind of miss the conversations
About our city and these changes
The displacement of the seniors
The ordaining of the Caesar
And the Quickening of fever
Pitching ideas over wood oven pizza
And the coolest craft malt liquor
Us fools!
We should have thought bigger
When the land was cheaper
The collective attention skewed eastern
This was our secret, raw speck of dust
On the palm of Michigan
And on that speck
We was living microscopic
Simple dreams and sin

Now
20 years later
On my 39th birthday
I remember 19
Being one of the fresh kids
Who now have children
Who stop in the Starbucks
And consume this convenience
I never thought would come

Could call it a progress
I'll call it a sure thing
Wide open for the right ones
With paper of green

This is for the brother
Jean jacket, a million buttons
The King of Cass
Adorned is his crown

And to all young the misfits
Promise to enjoy it!
Treat each alley like it's sacred
Please, pick up your garbage

Hop on the gentri-train
Pop in the new pop ups
But respect the bumpy road
Underneath the bike lane

Cass Corridor
The original name.

# Cass Corridor

## Elias Khalil

ounded on the south by the Fisher, the north by the Ford, the west by the Lodge, and the east by M-1 (a.k.a. Woodward) lies the neighborhood and state of mind known as the Cass Corridor. Welcome.

One hundred years ago, the Cass Corridor was an exclusive residential area, replete with Victorian mansions and Gothic-inspired churches, within walking distance of the burgeoning downtown. As the city grew rapidly in the 1920s, the Corridor—a transition zone on the northern edge of the central business district—became home to short-term housing and automotive-related businesses that fundamentally changed the character of the area. The affluent moved further north, and the housing stock began to be neglected.

Urban renewal projects after World War II accelerated this change. The building of the Fisher and Lodge Freeways literally eliminated whole portions of the neighborhood, creating new boundaries for the Cass Corridor. City leaders in the 1960s relocated the poorest residents from downtown's Skid Row to the neighborhood. Wayne State University and Medical Center expansions in the 1960s and 1970s leveled other residential areas. These disruptions were a blow to the then-working-class population, creating the perfect storm for the Cass Corridor to become the hub of crime, drug activity, prostitution, blight, and homelessness for an entire generation.

In the midst of these metamorphoses, and the great societal events of the Civil Rights Movement and the Vietnam War, Wayne State University remained the city's largest higher education institution, serving as a magnet for students and citizens across the spectrum of interests and ideologies. Progressives, radicals, nonconformists, artists, musicians, and anarchists of every race, color, creed, and orientation made the Cass Corridor their home. This diversity made and continues to make the Cass Corridor one of Detroit's richest cradles of culture and creativity.

The advent of the twenty-first century brought renewed interest in the area by the University Cultural Center Association (UCCA) to create an alliance among the major commercial, educational, cultural, and medical institutions. This alliance became the driving force for the redevelopment of the area, also expanding the targeted geographical footprint to encompass areas north and east of the Cass Corridor. This zone is the recently rebranded sector now known as Midtown Detroit.

So, what is a neighborhood? For me, it's not just a space. It's a place. A place that derives its meaning from the people who inhabit it. The interplay of people within a place defines our love for it.

Anyone can walk down a street and visit a building anywhere—in Detroit, in Paris, or in Dakar. Yet what makes it a desirable destination is the story of that place: the people, the personalities, and the relationships.

And the Cass Corridor neighborhood is an amazing place! It's full of some of the most interesting people in the city. These people have built, maintained, rebuilt, and enriched their neighborhood, defining and authoring its evolution over the decades. The Cass Corridor has a great history: once the city's wealthiest residential area; home to the world's first auto show in the Willys-Overland building; a national hub for film distribution, pharmaceuticals, and automotive parts suppliers; home to the largest Masonic Temple in the United States; home to one of the oldest family-owned liquor licenses in Detroit, through George at the Temple Bar; home to Dally in the Alley, the studio and stage for Marcus Belgrave, Jack White, Joni Mitchell, and many more.

The people and personalities of the last few decades have defined the Cass Corridor of our time. Who are these people? They are risk-takers, courageous blue-collar hustlers, solidarity-minded good Samaritans, helping hands, and nonconformists. They are off the grid, artistically expressive, intelligent, savvy, cosmopolitan, global, color blind. They are committed to affordability, access, inclusivity, safety, cleanliness, pedestrian and bike-friendly environments, local sourcing, recycling, ecological responsibility, and cultural diversity. These people do not wait for others to deliver; they act. In their environment—often viewed by others as blighted, distressed, and disposable—they create their own beauty and desired reality. A beauty those who remain in gated communities will never experience. We who live, work, and play in the Cass Corridor do so deliberately. This is our home. We are happy here. We have created an enviable community and quality of life only dreamt about by others.

We have assets like other great neighborhoods that we would love for you to check out. Our greatest assets, though, are the residents and business owners. As you come to our home, you'll meet the following people. When you get to know us, you'll know what roles we play in making our neighborhood so wonderful. Dell and Sharon, Nefertiti, Janet, James and Jason, Faith, Chuck, Donny, German Phil, Ray, Paul, Chris, Charlene, Scott and Caroline, John and Dan, Allen, Carol, Shannon and Matt and Adriel, Elias and Pilar, Dan, Liz, George and Victor, Akbar, Joel, Ralph, Moritz, Kim, Simone, Adnan, Bob, Felicia, Michelle and Joe, Cedric and Nu, Ann and Atiba and Leslie and Glenn and Jackie, Tom and Peggy and Jason, Emily and Andy, Sarge, George, Cindy, Pat, Austin, Peter and Michael.

Want music (with possible dancing)? Check out the Masonic Temple, the Old Miami, the Temple Bar, Tony V's. Want theater? Check out the Hilberry. Want art? Check out Galerie Camille, the Simone DeSousa Gallery, Dell Pryor Gallery, the DAM, the Elaine L. Jacob Gallery, the Robert Sestok City Sculpture Park. Want a local brewery? Check out Motor City Brewing Works, Traffic Jam and Snug. Want a bar or beer? Check out the Bronx, Jumbos, Third Street, Lefty's Lounge, Circa Saloon, Honest John's, 8° Plato. Want great food? Check out La Feria Spanish Tapas, Goodwells, the Cass Café, Avalon, Shangri-La, Selden Standard, Byblos, Harmonie Garden, Go Sy Thai, Slows To Go, Peterboro, Mario's. Want cool gifts? Check out Tulani Rose, Source Booksellers, City Bird, Nest, Hugh, Nora. Want pet care? Check out Canine to Five, Cass Corridog. Want clothes? Check out Flo Boutique, Detroit Clothing Co. Want a bike? Check out the Hub. Want Hair Care? Textures by Nefertiti, the Social Club Grooming Company. Want a hardware store or keys? Third Avenue, Fred's Key Shop. Need social services? Check out Cass Corridor Neighborhood Development Corporation, Mariners Inn, Cass Community Social Services, and the Children's Center. Want local history and photography? Find Ralph Rinaldi or Kim Schroeder, or visit the Reuther Library. Need great high schools? Go to Detroit School of the Arts, Cass Technical High School. Want to start a business? Meet Sue Mosey. And this list is far from exhaustive.

The Cass Corridor is constantly changing, constantly evolving: like every neighborhood and every city, like us as individuals, like life itself.

# Tiger Stadium

## *Vince Guerrieri*

*T*he first time I was ever at a place where history came up through the ground and reached me was when I stood on the field at Tiger Stadium before its last opening day in 1999.

I'm a little embarrassed to admit that. Our family vacations were always to some historic site—a testament as much to my mother's desire to have some type of educational value as to my father's nearly pathological fear of water. I stood on the Boston Common. We walked the battlefield at Gettysburg, saw the homes of George Washington and Thomas Jefferson, and toured Fort McHenry.

But standing on the field at Tiger Stadium, where baseball had been played for more than a century, I drank it all in. Alan Trammell stood on the dugout steps signing autographs. Gene Budig, the president of the American League, was giving interviews. And I had my Patton-at-the-Carthaginian-battlefield moment. There was the transformer Reggie Jackson bounced a moon shot off of in the 1971 All-Star Game. There was the spot in left field where Ducky Medwick was pelted with abuse in the 1934 World Series, and removed from the game by the commissioner—as much for his safety as anything else. Lou Gehrig's consecutive game streak ended here. Joe Louis fought here. The Detroit Lions won NFL titles here. Nelson Mandela spoke here. Anyone of any repute since the founding of the American League—and more than a few National Leaguers (Tiger Stadium hosted seven World Series and three All-Star Games)—played here.

And within a year, it would be left to rot.

I grew up in Youngstown, a city in Ohio almost on the Pennsylvania border, equidistant from Cleveland and Pittsburgh. Every year as a family, we'd go to baseball games at Three Rivers Stadium or Municipal Stadium. Later on, we went to Progressive Field, a shimmering new baseball-only park that opened in time to coincide with the best era of Indians baseball since the early 1950s.

But Tiger Stadium was the first ballpark I visited that was mine alone. For many of my fellow students at Bowling Green, Windsor beckoned, with a casino, a drinking age of nineteen, and numerous adult entertainment establishments. For me, it was Detroit and Tiger Stadium.

Every ballpark has its own descriptor. Municipal Stadium in Cleveland was cavernous. Wrigley Field will always be the Friendly Confines, and thanks to John Updike, Fenway Park is a lyric little bandbox. Tiger Stadium—at least since owner Walter Briggs built a second deck that went all the way around the ballpark—was imposing. Players and fans alike said it looked like a beached battleship, looming over I-75 at the intersection of Michigan and Trumbull Avenues.

I got to my first game at Tiger Stadium in 1996. It offered an intimate viewing experience, particularly for its size, and the fireworks I saw there remain the best postgame show I've ever seen. But the stadium was already starting to near the end of the line, with talk of a new facility coming almost instantly after pizza magnate Tom Ilitch bought the team in 1992.

Most ballparks built in the sport's early years weren't in downtown areas. They weren't heralded as engines of economic development. They were built wherever the team owners could get enough land to put a baseball field. In Cleveland, it was at the end of a streetcar line at the corner of East Sixty-Sixth Street and Lexington Avenue. In Pittsburgh it was in the Oakland neighborhood, near the University of Pittsburgh. In New York City, it was Coogan's Bluff, overlooking the Harlem River.

And in Detroit, it was the corner of Michigan and Trumbull in Corktown. Settled by Irish immigrants in the 1850s, the name was already a misnomer by the time Charlie Bennett built a wooden grandstand in 1896 to accommodate crowds to watch the Detroit Tigers, then a minor-league team in the Western League. At the time, there was only one major league, the National League.

But in 1900, the Western League became the American League, and a year later became a major league, fielding teams in the National League cities of Boston, Philadelphia, and St. Louis, as well as in Cleveland, Washington, Milwaukee, Baltimore, and Detroit.

The sport grew in popularity, touching off a building boom of stadiums. The wooden grandstands were replaced by steel-and-concrete fireproof structures. In a three-year span, new ballparks sprouted up in Pittsburgh, Chicago, Washington D.C., Cleveland, and Detroit—all designed by the same company, Osborn Engineering of Cleveland.

The new stadium in Detroit would be built on the same site, at Michigan and Trumbull. Navin Field, named for the Tigers' owner, Frank Navin, opened on April 20, 1912, the same week the Titanic sank.

The city was booming, thanks to the nascent auto industry, and the ballpark expanded to accommodate that, from 24,000 when it opened, to 30,000 less than a decade later. It also added tenants. In 1934, the Portsmouth Spartans of the National Football League were bought by George Richards, the owner of WJR. He moved the team to Detroit, and playing off the baseball team's name, called them the Lions, saying that, as the lion was king of the jungle, they would soon be king of football.

After Navin's death in 1935, the team passed to Walter Briggs, who set about adding to the ballpark. Navin had added a second deck to the grandstand, but it was Briggs who enclosed the entire stadium, bringing capacity to 53,000, making Tiger Stadium the fourth largest baseball park in the major leagues.

And the teams won, too, coming home with a pennant in 1940 and a World Series win five years later. But for the two decades after that, the Tigers had the misfortune of not being as good as the Yankees. The most galling example came in 1961, when the Tigers won 101 games, but the Yankees won 109 to win the pennant in the days before divisions and a month-long baseball postseason.

But by the mid-1960s, the Yankees had sunk into mediocrity. In 1967, the year of riots in Detroit, the Red Sox beat the Tigers for the American League pennant on the last day of the season. The following year, they would they not be so denied, winning the pennant and the World Series.

But the riots at Twelfth and Grand River had started an exodus—including the city's football and basketball teams. During the early years of the NFL, many teams played in stadiums built by more established baseball teams. The Bears played for decades at Wrigley Field, the Giants called Yankee Stadium and the Polo Grounds home, and the Lions played at Tiger Stadium. But in 1975, the Silverdome opened, bigger and able to be used year-round (and, left unsaid, not in Detroit). The Lions made it their home, and the Pistons left the old Detroit Olympia and played there for a decade before building their new venue in Auburn Hills.

The Tigers had one more great year left at Tiger Stadium, leading wire-to-wire in 1984 and winning the American League East division before advancing to and winning the World Series. Five years later, the Tigers lost 103 games. It was the start of a lost decade, an ignominious ending for the stadium at the corner of Michigan and Trumbull.

In the 1990s, many of the structures that hailed from the original era of stadium construction in the early 1900s were an endangered species. Comiskey Park was torn down, replaced by a new, soulless stadium next door. George Steinbrenner rattled the saber about moving the Yankees to New Jersey, and there was talk of replacing Fenway Park in Boston.

Like those stadiums, Tiger Stadium was built without luxury boxes, and the amenities that had become standard in watching a game had to be foregone—or retrofitted at great cost.

One of Ilitch's previous projects had been the restoration of the venerable Fox Theater. Detroit's opulent theaters had been abandoned as multiplexes took over, or in the case of the Michigan, had been repurposed as a parking garage. The theater's location on Woodward Avenue had started to become an entertainment hub, and that's where the Tigers' new home would go as well, as would a new stadium for the Lions.

The Tigers moved into Comerica Park in 2000. As a baseball fan, I've been to old and new stadiums in five different cities: the Bronx in New York, Cleveland,

Pittsburgh, Cincinnati, and Detroit. Tiger Stadium's the only one I miss. The Lions moved into Ford Field four years later. Their respective previous venues were left behind.

Tiger Stadium's fate was debated. Does it get reused? What element of historical preservation would be made for the ballpark? And while it was debated, it sat—for another decade. Through the miracle of CGI, it became Yankee Stadium for Billy Crystal's movie *61\** about those 1961 Yankees that denied the 101-win Tigers the pennant. A tent was pitched on the field and it hosted Snoop Dogg's party when the Super Bowl came to Detroit in 2006. And its last appearance—days before demolition started—was in the backdrop of a scene in *Kill the Irishman*, a movie about a Cleveland mob war.

Tiger Stadium was torn down in 2009. Three years later, Fenway Park—which opened the same day Tiger Stadium did—was feted for its centennial. It had eluded the wrecking ball, and it became a hot spot after two World Series wins, lifting a putative "curse" that was sold to Boston fans who refused to deal with the fact that the team was hampered by its own segregation.

Today all that remains of Tiger Stadium on a site where baseball was played for a century is the 125-foot-tall flagpole.

# Steve's Place

*R.J. Fox*

On the loneliest street, in the loneliest city, Steve's Place was a lighthouse in an urban wasteland gone wild. The fresh blanket of snow that had fallen on the surrounding neighborhood had an almost heavenly, ethereal quality.

Adrift in the winter landscape were Jimmy and Julia Schicksal, who somehow managed to veer off track while driving home from a friend's birthday party at a downtown Detroit club, where they spent most of the evening pretending (wishing) that the other didn't exist. In recent months, fighting had become their only shared activity. Lately, most of their arguments were done in silence, which was often far worse than the ones filled with words.

They were so lost in their own individual—yet mutual—suffering, they had somehow roamed off course. The fact that the snow was now falling even harder certainly didn't help, making it nearly impossible to see a foot in front of them. Jimmy was prone to getting lost in normal driving conditions; one of the *many* faults Julia found with her husband. The list was growing exponentially by the day.

Sadly, it wasn't that long ago when Jimmy and Julia were frequently described by others as "the perfect couple." They were *that* good at keeping up the illusion when out in public. Lately, it was getting harder. Behind closed doors, their relationship was reduced to smoldering ruins. They tried counseling, but came to the conclusion that the only thing that succeeded in doing was draining their now separate bank accounts. It was no longer a matter of *if*. It was a matter of *when*...a foregone conclusion.

Jimmy looked over at Julia, who stared through the snow-covered windshield with a glare so sharp, it could cut glass. She finally ripped through the decaying silence like a dagger.

"How did this happen?" she asked.

"I must have taken a wrong turn," Jimmy said.

"Why am I not surprised?" Julia said with disdain. Jimmy's only response was to clench the steering wheel, knowing that remaining mute was in his best interest. Besides, Julia was right. He had the ability to get lost in his own neighborhood.

"Of all the places to get lost in, you had to pick here," Julia continued.

"It's not like I did it on purpose," Jimmy said, still gripping onto the wheel for both weather and spousal conditions.

"This is why I should have driven," Julia retorted.

"Well, if you didn't drink so much, then you could have," Jimmy said, struggling to keep his temper at a low simmer. "You obviously didn't notice that I was going the wrong way, either."

"You're the driver," Julia said.

"I'll figure it out," Jimmy said, without a speck of confidence. "I always do."

Jimmy looked around at his snow-diffused surroundings, consisting of abandoned skyscrapers and storefronts, punctuated with busted-out windows and graffiti. It was like being trapped in a snow globe from hell. Not a single streetlight worked. Not a soul was in sight, not even a prostitute or a homeless person. They might as well have been at the end of the world.

As Julia continued to fume, Jimmy continued to struggle with his attempt at creating the illusion that he had things under control, despite having no clue where he was. There was a reason why Julia normally drove. But after taking a drink tally, they determined Jimmy was the wiser choice that night. This was no surprise. Lately, Julia was turning more to booze to remedy her reality—at least more so than her husband.

"What are we going to do?" Julia continued to nag in that grating voice of hers, which once upon a time, Jimmy thought was the sweetest sound in the world.

"What would you like me to do?" Jimmy asked.

"Stop being such a fuck-up. That's what I want you to do."

Jimmy pretended to ignore this. He had heard it all before. However, deep inside him was another story. No matter how many times she called him a "fuck-up," "loser," and any other term of endearment du jour, her words stung on the outside, poisoning him slowly on the inside.

Meanwhile, the snow had begun to fall harder, making it harder to see in front of him. Panic began setting in, but he refused to show it. He truly had no idea how to get back on course and he imagined that getting lost in a Michigan snowstorm in the middle of downtown Detroit was about as close to hell on earth as one could get. But suddenly, straight ahead in the distance, an amber light appeared, burning through the falling snow.

"What is that?" Jimmy asked.

"Obviously, a light," Julia said.

"Maybe it'll be somewhere we can stop and ask for directions."

"Or get us killed," Julia countered.

"Do you have a better idea?"

She ignored him. Jimmy continued driving toward the snow-diffused light, which slowly revealed itself to be emanating from a green brick building with a matching green and white striped awning, which stood on an otherwise abandoned block with several long-shuttered buildings.

Jimmy parked along the curb in front of the decrepit building. It was difficult to fathom how any business could flourish in this location—both in terms of the building itself and its environs. One end of the structure's awning fluttered ghostlike in the wind. Peeling paint on the side of the building proclaimed "Steve's Place," below which said, "Fine Homemade Food. Cocktails. Open 7 Days." Despite the run-down outward appearance, there was something down home, warm, and inviting about this place. Then again, compared with the rest of the block, that wasn't saying much.

"This looks like a dump," said Julia.

"We needs directions," Jimmy countered. "Plus, I need a drink."

"We have beer at home," Julia reminded him.

"It's gone," Jimmy said, realizing he probably shouldn't have admitted that.

"Well, you're not getting a drink here. You're going to go in, get directions, and then leave so we can get the hell out of here so I can get to bed," Julia demanded in a tone that made it clear to him that she would have the bed to herself tonight.

"Okay, I won't get a drink. But I'm not leaving you out here," Jimmy said.

"As if you care."

"If I didn't care, then I wouldn't want you to come in with me."

"If you cared, you wouldn't have gotten lost in the first place," Julia said, forming her own sense of rationality.

Jimmy opted not to dignify her statement with a response.

"Are you sure they're even open?" Julia asked.

Jimmy peered through the falling snow and pointed to an "Open" sign in the window of the otherwise darkened bar.

"Then stop wasting time. Go in there and get it done."

"Okay, okay," Jimmy said, beginning to get out of the car. "You're not coming?"

"No. I already told you," Julia said.

Jimmy was too tired to argue anymore. He cautiously got out of the car to brave both the elements and the environment. His feet disappeared several inches into fluffy, freshly fallen snow. As he took one step toward the entrance, he felt a chill run through his entire body, unlike anything he ever felt before. He considered hightailing it back to the car, but before he could collect his thoughts and take another step, Julia got out of the car and joined him. Whatever he felt, he assumed she felt it, too. Her presence made the chill subside, though he could still feel its lingering effect.

"Scared?" Jimmy asked.

"Shut up," which Jimmy knew translated into "yes."

Jimmy smiled at her. It was the best he could do when she got like this, which infuriated her even more.

Jimmy reached for the rusty door handle, but it didn't budge.

"It's locked," Jimmy said.

"Are you sure?"

Jimmy tried again. "Yes. Pretty sure."

"Let me try," Julia said, nudging Jimmy out of the way. Sure enough it was locked.

"Well, this sucks," Julia said. "Now what?"

Jimmy peered through the window, partially obscured by blinds. Julia joined him. The well-stocked bar stood empty. Unlit Christmas lights were unevenly strung across the bar and around the entire perimeter of the building. Not a soul was in sight.

"Okay, let's go," Julia said. "It's obviously closed."

"But it says it's open," Jimmy insisted.

"This place is freaking me out. We'll figure out how to get home on our own."

Suddenly, a harsh wind blew, knocking a drift of snow from the roof, narrowly missing Jimmy and Julia down below.

"Look!" Jimmy said, pointing toward the door. Somehow, it creaked open.

"Must have been the wind?" Julia said.

"But it was firmly locked. Guess we're going in, after all." Jimmy entered, leaving Julia little choice but to relent and follow him with skeptical footing.

As though on cue, a scratchy recording of Billie Holiday's melancholy "Solitude" poured out of an ancient jukebox in front of the window, mingling with a musty odor that hinted of death and nostalgia. The cobwebbed Christmas lights also flickered on—first in struggling dimness, before surging to full life, blinking erratically. One thing was clear to Jimmy: these lights weren't put up for this Christmas, but rather some forgotten Christmas from long ago.

The entire bar felt abandoned, oozing a nauseating, musty smell that hinted of death. Various faded posters advertising beer and booze products punctuated the room. No one was there.

Jimmy and Julia situated themselves on swiveling, squeaky barstools with torn, faded, green vinyl padding. The coupled soaked in their unsettling surroundings, not uttering a word, as though breaking the silence would shatter the illusion of the surreal universe they just entered. Julia's expression suggested that this was the last place in the world she wanted to be. Jimmy, on the other hand, was enthralled by their discovery. He felt as though they had entered into another dimension of time and space.

Despite the lonely, suffocating sound of a hissing, rattling radiator, the bar was cold as death itself. Jimmy removed his coat, but Julia kept hers on. She was always cold to begin with—this place certainly wasn't going to change that.

"Can you believe this place?" Jimmy asked, finally breaking the silence. The illusion remained.

"Were you expecting anything different?" Julia asked.

"I'm not complaining. I think this place is awesome."

"Well, clearly nobody is here, so why don't we get going?"

"Maybe I can help myself to a beer and leave money on the bar," Jimmy said.

"You can't do that," Julia said.

"Why not? It's not like I'm stealing it."

Just as "Solitude" reached its lonely conclusion, shuffling footsteps were heard from above. Jimmy and Julia waited in suspense. Moments later, the footsteps began a slow descent down an unseen staircase. After what felt like an eternity, a door at the back of the bar buried in shadow opened up and out of the darkness came a gaunt, elderly man in a plaid shirt. Jimmy found the sight both equally haunting and comical. One look at Julia's horrified face was all Jimmy needed to hold back his stifled laughter as the haunted man continued to advance toward the bar. He moved at a snail's pace, hunched over from a lifetime of weariness. His feet never once left the ground, but instead, shuffled along the faded black and red tiled floor, worn and beaten by time itself.

As the bartender crept nearer, Jimmy once again felt the chill he experienced outside the bar. Jimmy noticed Julia tighten up with fear as the bartender proceeded to walk right past them…as though they weren't there at all. He headed straight to the jukebox and turned on a neon light bordering the window, through which the snow had begun falling even harder. As the bartender slowly made his way back to the bar, The Eurythmics' "Sweet Dreams (Are Made of This)" came on. Steve smiled and nodded his along to the music. Steve's Place was now officially open for business.

When he finally came to his resting place behind the bar in front of Jimmy and Julia, he buckled over with a violent, bronchial cough, before finally struggling to regain his breath.

"Something to drink?" the bartender finally asked, in a thick, unrecognizable accent. He proceeded to adjust the collar of his plaid shirt, which was buttoned to the very top. It was faded and torn, neatly tucked all the way into his pants, which were pulled up high above his twisted, thin waist. His peppered hair was neatly combed, and still wet with either or gel—or perhaps both.

"What do you have on tap?" Jimmy asked.

Julia gave her husband a characteristic glare for even entertaining the bartender's offer. Although he would never admit it, Jimmy knew his wife was right. He didn't need another drink any more than she did. Like arguing, drinking was one of the few things they had in common anymore—though it was usually done in separate rooms. Or locations all together.

"No tap. Bottles. Just Stroh's," the bartender said.

The bartender ended every sentence with the smacking of his dry, chapped lips. His musty breath poured out of his partially shaven faced. It smelled much like the bar itself, as though the two were somehow one and the same.

"That's it?" Jimmy asked, disappointed in his beer options.

"That's it," the bartender replied matter of factly.

"Then I guess I'll have a Stroh's."

The bartender turned toward Julia.

"You?"

"Nothing, thanks," Julia replied, looking right at Jimmy with her patented death glare.

"No drink, then you must leave," the bartender said.

"Seriously?" Julia asked. Jimmy chuckled, pissing Julia off even more.

"Yes," Steve said, with a stern glare. "You want drink, you stay. No drink, you go. So drink then, yes?"

Julia realized she didn't have much of a choice. She was too tired to try picking a fight with this man. Jimmy was surprised she surrendered so quickly. In the past, Julia always stood her ground in situations such as this. It saddened Jimmy to see her so resigned to her fate.

"Bud?" the bartender asked.

"Bud."

"Would you like my wife to fix you something?" the bartender said.

"I'm sorry, what?" Jimmy asked

"Would you like my wife to fix you something?" the bartender repeated with more enunciation, which did little to clarify what he was trying to express. He made an eating motion with his hand to his mouth.

"Eat?"

"Oh. As in food!" Jimmy said, looking at Julia, who was staring past the bar, where a row of dust-covered lime-green booths lined each side of the room, leading to an abandoned kitchen littered with dirty pots and pans from a meal served long ago.

"Want something?" Jimmy asked.

Julia flashed Jimmy a look that suggested "Are you crazy?"

Clues leading to what may have last been prepared in that kitchen hung behind the bar on a plastic signboard, featuring weekly menu options posted in plastic letter pins—many of which were missing:

Mon: Ro st B ef/Chi k n Noo le

u s: Ro st Chi ken/Na y B an

We : Me balls & Spa.

Thur: Sh rt Rib / t Pea

ri. Fi h & Chi s/Cl am Ch wde

"Food, yes?" the bartender asked.

"Just beer's fine," Jimmy said, characteristically caving in, wondering if refusal would be grounds for removal.

With a sad, puppy-dogged face, the bartender got to work, retrieving two beer bottles out of an old, grimy fridge. As Chet Baker continued to croon his troubles away, the bartender moved in the deliberate manner of a sloth. No one said a word—only Chet, as though demanding to be heard. His lyrics said it all.

Jimmy noticed a faded calendar from 1983 hanging on the wall. Seemingly random, off-kilter knick-knacks from decades past were scattered on both the bar and shelves above the bar. Even the bottles of liquor appeared dated beyond their faded labels. Behind the bar rested an antique cash register that was probably older than the bar itself.

As the bartender finally popped the tops off with a rusty bottle opener, Julia removed her coat. The place was slowly, but surely, beginning to warm up.

With trembling hands, the bartender slowly set the beer bottles down on the severely scratched blue, faux-wood bar, which was peeling off in every possible direction with edges accentuated with green, tattered, and torn vinyl padding. Two shot glasses suddenly joined the beer bottles.

"Oh, just beer's fine," Jimmy said.

"Comes with beer," the bartender said.

"It's free?" Julia asked.

"Not free," the bartender replied. "On me…on me."

"Okay, I'll have, um, a shot of whiskey," Jimmy said.

"Peach Schnapps. That's it," the bartender scolded.

"Okay. Then Peach Schnapps it is," Jimmy said with a confused chuckle.

"Good choice," the bartender said with a sly smile, before pouring them some. Despite his shaky hand, he managed to fill Jimmy's glass up till the very brim, without spilling a single drop. When he attempted to fill Julia's glass, she put her hand over it in an effort to stop him.

"No thanks," Julia said, but the bartender insisted.

"Peach Schnapps. Very good, very good," he said, tilting the bottle toward her glass. Julia moved her hand out of the way just in the nick of time. Another surrender.

When the bartender was done pouring, he put the bottle back, then reached for a bottle of whiskey, which he proceeded to pour for himself, drawing a shared smile between Jimmy and Julia—something Jimmy assumed was a thing of the past. Judging from Julia's expression, she felt the same way. For once, they were on the same page. As much as it felt good, it felt even stranger.

The bartender then held up his glass and proclaimed, "To old times," a refrain that both Jimmy and Julia repeated. They then all downed their shots, as though they were old friends. Jimmy proceeded to take a sip of his beer. He cringed, nearly spitting it out.

"It's warm!" Jimmy said.

"Fridge broke. Can't fix," the bartender said in defense.

"Maybe you should get a repairman in here?"

The bartender merely shrugged. It wasn't clear whether the shrug implied indifference…or confusion. It was quite possible that no repairman would venture this far into the urban wilderness even if called upon. That was probably the more likely explanation.

"So, are you the owner?" Jimmy asked.

"Yes," the bartender said in reply. "And wife."

"Then does that make you Steve?" Jimmy asked.

"Yes. Stefano. My wife, she Sofia. She sleep upstairs."

"You live here?" Jimmy asked, genuinely curious about this strange man and his strange bar.

"Yes."

"Where are you from?"

"We come from Greece."

"How long have you owned this place?"

"Thirty-two years," Steve said with pride.

"Wow," Julia said. "That's a long time."

"This place," began Steve. "My life. My joy. My jail."

"If you don't mind my asking, how old are you?"

"I was born forty-seven years ago."

"You're forty-seven?!" Jimmy asked. Seventy-five would have been too young of a guess.

"If you want to know the truth, I really don't know," Steve added.

"You don't know how old you are?" Julia said.

Steve shrugged, then added, "You sure you don't want something fixed?"

"Other than the fridge?" Jimmy joked. "We're fine. We already ate."

Not satisfied with Jimmy's answer, Steve looked toward Julia. "You?"

Just then, a cockroach raced across the bar past Jimmy and Julia. Julia shrieked. The bartender either didn't hear, notice, or ignored the situation altogether.

"Nope. We're good."

Disappointed, Steve took the shot glasses away and turned his back away from them. He proceeded to carefully remove a small sheet of paper from his shirt pocket, followed by dried herbs of some sort that he kept in an envelope.

"Is that weed?" Julia whispered to Jimmy.

"I'm assuming maybe tobacco?" Jimmy said, as Steve started to gently roll his own cigarette, before removing a book of matches from his pants pocket, which he used to light his handmade cigarette.

"Smoke?" Steve asked, taking a long drag.

"No thanks," Jimmy said. "But can you please tell me where the restroom is?"

"In back. You'll find easy," Steve said, taking another puff, which led to another coughing fit.

"Thanks," Jimmy said, getting up from his stool just as Johnny Cash's "I'd Just be Fool Enough (to Fall)" cried out of the jukebox.

"Don't leave me alone with him," Julia whispered in a plea to her husband.

"I'll be quick," Jimmy assured her.

"Another reason you need to stop drinking. You piss too much."

"You bitch too much," Jimmy retorted. "That's another reason to drink." Though she was pissed, Jimmy noticed a layer of hurt beneath her tough exterior. Unable to bear the sight of it, Jimmy headed toward the restroom, slipping into the darkness and instantly regretting what he said—as was usually the case…as was being too stubborn to ever apologize. Perhaps tonight would be different.

Jimmy cautiously walked past the kitchen—noticing a sink filled with dirty dishes that appeared to have been there for several days—if not weeks. Their decision not to order food was certainly a wise one.

Jimmy passed the door Steve entered through upon his arrival and felt the same, odd chill he felt earlier, mixed with his increasing guilt for what he said to Julia. It formed quite the eerie cocktail. Jimmy quickened his pace and continued walking down a dark red hallway with a single, flickering light, just barely illuminating the various broken bottles and abandoned junk littering the edges of the hallway.

He finally entered the men's room consisting of one trough urinal and one stall with a missing door. It was even darker inside the restroom than it was in the hallway.

Jimmy scrambled to find a light switch, but it didn't work. The only light source came from a busted, barred window located next to the trough. In the center of the trough was a round Hanoi Jane sticker, featuring Jane Fonda's face, illuminated by the same amber light that drew them to the bar to begin with.

As Jimmy took aim at his target, he continued to ruminate not only over what he said to Julia, but over everything he ever did to hurt her—big or small. He wished he could go take it all back and go back to the start. It saddened him that he couldn't.

A cold wind suddenly rushed through the window, carrying with it several snow-flakes that landed on his exposed flesh. Despite the frosty air, Jimmy found it refreshing compared to the musty air suffocating the rest of the bar. It rejuvenated his senses and partially cleared his clouded, muddled mind.

When he finished the showering of Hanoi Jane, he approached the rusty sink, containing the nasty, caked remnants of a bar of soap glued to the ledge. Jimmy opted to skip the soap, rinsing his hands instead—although the thought of turning the rusty, scum-covered handle wasn't exactly a consolation prize. His concerns were amplified by the fact that the handle wouldn't budge. After a brief struggle, he finally managed to loosen it, unleashing a rush of rusty water. He waited several seconds for the water to clear up, rinsed his hands, then turned toward the towel dispenser, which he realized was a dirty, yellowed cloth towel.

As Jimmy dried his hands on his pants, the toilet flushed behind him. He turned around to face the doorless stall just in time to see the remainder of the rusty water spiraling down the filthy bowl. Freaked out, he scampered the hell out of there, running down the dark hallway, tripping over a discarded milk crate, and falling hard to the filthy, grimy ground. He took a moment to make sure he wasn't seriously injured. Aside from a couple of bruises, he was fine. He got back onto his feet, looked behind him to make sure he wasn't being followed, and then tried his best to regain his composure before Julia came back into view. But it was no use.

"What happened to you?" Julia asked.

"Just got a little spooked, that's all," Jimmy said. "Julia, about what I said earlier, I'm sor—"

"You look like you a saw a ghost," Steve interrupted with a sly smile.

"I may have," Jimmy said.

"Another shot?" Steve asked, reaching for the bottle of Peach Schnapps.

"No, thanks. I really shouldn't."

"Schnapps, good," Steve said.

"Yes, very good," Jimmy agreed. "Which is why you should save it for others… or yourself."

"Never runs out," Steve said with a wink.

"So do you get a lot of customers in here?" Jimmy asked, in an attempt to divert the conversation.

"Sometime yes. Sometime no," Steve said. "When there event, many come. No event, few. Trouble. So…much…trouble."

"And you've stayed in business all these years?" Jimmy asked

"Don't need money," Steve continued. "People come, they come. They don't, they don't. No difference. Work is home and home is work. We need nothing."

Jimmy attempted to soak in everything Steve was telling them, but the more he thought about it, the less sense he could make of it all. Julia appeared equally perplexed.

Without warning, Steve suddenly shouted "Go away!!" while shaking his fist toward the window. Jimmy and Julia saw a couple of African American women peering through the window. Steve continued to fume, shaking his head in frustration. The warm, genteel host somehow morphed into a raving lunatic.

Meanwhile, the women acted like they didn't even notice Steve as they continued peering through the window, much in the way Jimmy and Julia were earlier.

"Not open!" Steve shouted. The women finally walked away. Steve shook his fist up in the air again, as though cursing God Himself. He muttered something indecipherable—in either English or Greek. Jimmy and Julia flashed one another a perplexed glance as Steve kept looking out the window in a paranoid fashion, his anger now reduced to a low simmer.

However, his anger completely dissipated the moment the haunting opening strings of Nat King Cole's "Stardust" flowed out of the jukebox, accompanied by shuffling footsteps up above beginning a slow journey down the steps.

While Jimmy and Julia waited in suspense, Steve beamed with excitement and anticipation in the direction of the door he earlier arrived in. After what felt like an eternity, the door finally opened and a ghostly woman appeared in a red and white polka-dotted nightgown, a beacon of light in the pitch black of the entranceway.

"That's my Sofia," Steve said with pride and a love so deep it inspired a strange sense of envy in Jimmy. He looked over at Julia and could instantly tell she felt the same.

As she shuffled zombielike across the floor from the back of the bar, she emerged out of the shadow and into the light, her lifeless eyes zeroing in on her husband as though nothing else in the world existed. Steve stood waiting for her at the end of the bar. When she finally reached him, he helped her into a tattered chair that was padded with an enormous pillow, proceeding to retrieve her a can of Vernors ginger ale from the warm fridge. He popped the top and handed it to her, once again in the fashion of a sloth. In comparison, her movements made Steve look like an Olympic sprinter. She reached for the can in the same manner, then took a long, slow sip. Her expression never changed. And her eyes never left her husband.

As Steve jaunted over to the jukebox, there seemed to be an extra spring in his step. He finally reached the jukebox just as "Stardust" ended. As he deliberately punched in his next selection, the bar hummed with the sound of the dying radiator and the buzz of shoddy electrical work. Although the radiator still sounded broken, it was now generating perhaps too much heat after a slow start.

As Steve made his way back toward his beloved Sofia, Patsy Cline's "Crazy" kicked in on the jukebox, which now sounded louder than before, echoing through the empty bar.

Steve reached his arm toward Sofia, even though she was still far from his reach. She reached out in return. Jimmy glanced at Julia, who smiled at him warmly. He couldn't remember the last time she looked at him like that.

As Steve honed in on his Sofia, their eyes locked in a loving embrace. Her dead eyes were now overflowing with life. To Jimmy, the couple now appeared younger, but he dismissed it as an illusion. When Steve finally reached her, he took her by the hand and helped her up before they began to dance to Patsy Cline's haunting, melancholy melody.

As Steve and Sofia danced, it was as though the rest of the world no longer mattered—or perhaps never existed at all. A lifetime of shared love, happiness, tears, and loss radiated from their beings, directly into Jimmy and Julia. As the dance progressed, Jimmy felt the negative feelings that had controlled him for so long slowly begin to erode until they were replaced by the old, happy feelings that had been packed away. They were now renewed and refreshed.

Meanwhile, the ancient couple danced and gazed at one another with a love so deep, it transcended human understanding. Jimmy could now clearly see just how far he and Julia had drifted apart from one another. He wondered whether once this moment was over, if they could somehow find a way to permanently return to where they once were and retrieve the towel they had thrown away so long ago. As they sat there and watched the embodiment of true love slowly being revealed right before their eyes, Jimmy began to fear that once the song was over, they would slip back to the dark void they were in when they first walked into the bar. There was nothing Jimmy wanted more than for this moment to last. Forever. Just like he thought it would seven years before when they both uttered, "I do."

Suddenly, Jimmy found himself on the brink of tears—the edges of which he saw forming in Julia's eyes. They turned to face one another at the same moment and without speaking a single word, Jimmy knew she was feeling exactly the same way. He reached for her hand. For once, she allowed him to take it into his. He felt his body fill with that old familiar feeling from a time when holding hands meant so much. Before it became meaningless, then an annoyance, then nonexistent.

Jimmy and Julia smiled at another and continued to do so through a cascade of falling tears. They were Jimmy & Julia again, rather than Jimmy and Julia—or more specifically. Jimmy. And Julia.

When they turned back to look at Steve and Sofia, the old couple had magically transformed into the exact age of Jimmy and Julia. It wasn't an illusion, Jimmy thought to himself. Or was it? Age was no longer relevant to this timeworn couple. Jimmy looked at Julia and she appeared to him exactly as she did on their wedding night, both in terms of her appearance and his feelings for her. It saddened him to think how once upon a time, he assumed he would always feel this way about her. He never imagined that the day would come when such a familiar feeling felt so… foreign.

Julia squeezed Jimmy's hand even tighter. He never wanted her to let go. Of this moment. Of him. Of them.

Steve suddenly waved Jimmy and Julia over to join them.

"Want to dance?" Jimmy asked Julia.

"Can we just stay like this?" Julia asked.

Jimmy nodded, gently caressing her held hand with his fingers. Steve persisted that they join them. Jimmy politely shook his head no.

At the song's key change, Steve dipped Sofia back. They not only remained young, but were suddenly bathed in a heavenly, ethereal light—a light that Jimmy felt permeating through both himself and through Julia, whose hand he still held.

As the song finally came to an end, they transformed back into their old selves, as Sofia buried her face into Steve's shoulder. Steve held her closely against him, as though fighting off the reality that the song was coming to an end—like everything else in life. Knowing this, they did not let go of one another until the echo of the very last note faded, absorbing into the very walls that held on to everything else that slipped from the present and into the past.

Steve kissed Sofia's hand and then watched as she slowly shuffled back to the door from which she came, out of the light, into shadow, and then back into darkness, until all that remained were the sound of her footsteps slowly ascending the stairs until coming to a rest.

Julia slowly let go of Jimmy's hand. All he could see on her face was sadness—the same sadness he felt inside.

As "Stardust" picked up where it left off, Steve turned back to Jimmy and Julia. "That's my Sofia," he beamed, before breaking into another violent coughing episode. Still coughing, he managed to pour himself some whiskey. He downed it, settling his cough.

"Another shot?" Steve asked.

"No, thanks," Julia said in a melancholy tone.

"I'm fine," Jimmy said, offering Julia a reassuring smile. Her face lightened.

"Have another," Steve insisted. "On me."

"No, seriously. We're good," Jimmy said. "We still have to drive."

Disappointed, Steve took the shot glasses away as Jimmy and Julia took a long sip of their beer. Steve regained his composure and smiled at them.

"Beautiful people," he said. "Beautiful people."

"Thank you," Julia said, flattered.

Jimmy finished his beer and Steve leaned against the bar.

"Stay in love," Steve began. Jimmy put his arm around Julia's shoulder just like he always used to do before her body language forced him give it up altogether. Now, she leaned in closer to him than ever before.

"Love lasts forever. Life does not. It is why there's no greater thing. And just like that, everything will be fine. Everything will be fine. Because love will always melt away all the snow."

Jimmy glanced at Julia, who smiled warmly at him as Billie Holiday's "I'll Be Seeing You" began a mournful lament out of the jukebox.

"Ready?" Jimmy finally said, looking toward the window. It was no longer snowing.

Julia nodded, taking one last sip of her beer.

"How much?" Jimmy asked Steve.

"On the house," Steve said, catching both by surprise. After all, Steve had already given them so much that night.

"Are you sure?" Jimmy asked.

"Don't need the monies anymore," Steve explained. "You keep it."

Jimmy set down a $10 bill.

With a shaking hand, Steve handed the money back to Jimmy.

"No tip. Keep it."

Jimmy refused to take the money back, but Steve insisted.

"Buy her something nice," said Steve, winking at Julia. Jimmy was left with no choice but to take it back. He could tell Steve was relieved.

"Thanks, Steve," Julia said.

"Yes. Welcome," Steve said in reply. "Beautiful people always welcome."

Jimmy and Julia stood up. Jimmy offered to help Julia put her coat on. Jimmy was pretty sure he caught her blushing.

"Thank you," Julia said.

"My pleasure," Jimmy replied back, before kissing her gently on the forehead as Steve watched with great satisfaction.

"Goodbye, Steve," Jimmy said.

"Yia sou," Steve said in Greek, before translating. "Goodbye, my friends."

Jimmy and Julia started to make their way toward the door, when Julia stopped in her tracks.

"We forgot to ask for directions!"

They turned back to Steve, but he was gone.

Suddenly, a booming voice commanded: "Okay, guys. Party's over." Just then, the jukebox, radiator, and every light in the place all shut off at once, as though somebody pulled a giant, invisible plug.

Jimmy and Julia turned toward the door, where a portly cop stood, revealing his badge.

"I'm sorry?" Jimmy said in confusion.

"You're trespassing," the cop said.

"Trespassing?" Jimmy said. "We're customers."

"That's what they all say," the officer said, annoyed.

"Just ask Steve," Jimmy said, turning toward where Steve was just standing. All that remained were two empty beer bottles.

"Come on, you two," the cop said, with his back already turned toward the door.

Jimmy and Julia followed the officer out in a state of confusion. Not only had it stopped snowing, it also felt much warmer.

"If I catch you in there again, you'll be arrested, do you understand me?" the cop warned, pointing an accusatory finger at them.

"Yes," Jimmy said, trying everything in his power to not question authority, despite the million questions running through his head.

The officer proceeded to put a thick padlock on the door. Jimmy could no longer bite his tongue.

"When you said 'that's what they all say,' what did you mean by that?"

The officer looked up into the night sky, as though searching for an answer, then sighed deeply.

"With all these empty buildings downtown, we periodically catch trespassers trying to salvage what's left. I don't know what it is about this place in particular, but there isn't a night that goes by where we don't find someone in here. Must be some kind of cheap thrill."

"But we were invited in by the owner, Steve...unless he was a trespasser, too?"

"It's always the same with you people," the cop said in a somber tone.

"We don't understand," Jimmy said.

"You know damn well what happened in here," the cop insisted.

"I'm sorry, Officer, but we really don't," Julia said.

The cop finally realized that they were telling the truth and took another deep sigh.

"About thirty years ago, the owners—who lived in the apartment upstairs for over thirty years—were robbed and murdered inside there. They've been closed ever since."

Jimmy felt that old familiar chill shoot through his body, stronger than ever.

"Which is why I implore you to STAY THE FUCK OUT!" the cop's voice echoed into the empty night. He turned around and walked away, leaving Jimmy and Julia to ponder their new reality. He disappeared around a corner, as though he were never there at all—much like Steve himself.

Jimmy and Julia were left with nothing but confused silence, haunted by loss. Still too stunned to speak, they both looked back toward the bar and noticed that in place of the "Open" sign was a "Closed" sign. The same chill Jimmy felt throughout the night returned—but intensified.

They peered through the window one last time, still unable to fathom what had just transpired.

The bar was still empty. And dark. Only the cobwebs remained, which led the eye to a framed photograph of Steve and Sofia dancing together on their wedding day—the only beacon of light remaining in the entire bar, looking just as they appeared while they were dancing just moments ago.

"Let's get home," Julia said, without a hint of the demanding tone she used earlier.

"We never did get directions, did we?" Jimmy realized.

"I'm sure we can figure it out," Julia said. "You eventually always do."

As they walked toward the car, Julia took Jimmy by the hand for the first time in months, as the remaining snow melted all around them.

# Jos. Campau Avenue and Parke-Davis Historic Site

*Heather Harper*

Tucked away outside of bustling downtown Detroit is a path less trodden on the Jos. Campau Avenue entrance to the Detroit RiverWalk. The street is named after a prominent Detroit man, Joseph Campau. In 1708, his grandfather, Jacques Campau, moved to Detroit from Montreal at the invitation of Antoine de la Mothe, Sieur de Cadillac, the man who founded the village seven years earlier in 1701. Not too far from Jos. Campau is John R Road, a street bearing the name of Joseph Campau's nephew, John R. Williams, the first mayor of Detroit (1824-1825).

Despite his importance to the growth of the city of Detroit in the nineteenth century, Joseph Campau has a tarnished legacy, as he was also a documented slave owner. After slavery was banned in 1787 by the Northwest Ordinance, the number of slaves in the Detroit area dwindled. But in 1805, nearly twenty years after the Northwest Ordinance, Campau was known to employ ten slaves of his own. Notably, the Sibley House of Detroit reports Joseph Campau was not permitted to be buried in Mount Elliot cemetery because he was excommunicated by the Catholic Church before he died.

A historical marker at Le Cote' Du Nord-Est is evidence of the Campau family's privilege and importance in the Detroit area. After being occupied by the Campau family for many generations, the site became headquarters of Parke-Davis and Company in 1874. The pharmaceutical research company campus comprised several buildings, some of which were designed by famed architect, Albert Kahn. The fourteen-and-a-half-acre complex housed the first pharmaceutical research lab to be built in the United States.

Nearly a century later, the Stroh family of the Stroh Brewery Company purchased the plant in 1979 from Parke-Davis. The Parke-Davis Research Laboratory complex is now listed on the National Register of Historic Places. Presently, the cluster of buildings is divided into Stroh River Place and Talon Center, which house apartments, offices, a hotel, and a restaurant. The architectural style is known as Romanesque Revival.

Nowadays, Jos. Campau is a destination where locals spend time wandering about on a sunny day. This section of the Detroit RiverWalk is a perfect place to get outside and enjoy the beauty of Detroit. A great day tour would be to start at Diamond Jack's River Tours over on Atwater Street and take a cruise on the Diamond Belle. After the tour, you can rent a bike from Wheelhouse Detroit at the same location and slow roll your way on over to Atwater Brewery, on Jos. Campau and Wight Street, to grab a local brew and delicious pub food while checking out the art gallery or playing a board game with the kids.

If you would rather get a little more use out of your bicycle rental, the RiverWalk runs approximately two miles from Wheelhouse Detroit to Mt. Elliott Park, which offers a large green space to take a break in. On your return trip, relax and take in a show at Chene Park Amphitheatre or visit William G. Milliken State Park and Harbor to see the authentic lighthouse. The Cullen Family Carousel is also stationed nearby, so be sure to take a quick peek (or ride) before you finish your tour. Created for Detroit, the carousel features hand-crafted sturgeon, egrets, and walleye, along with the mythical River Monster and River Mermaid. Rides cost $1 and proceeds benefit the Detroit Riverfront Conservancy.

# Seeking Solitude in Rivertown

*Jeff Waraniak*

For a city so supposedly empty, solitude can be hard to find in Detroit, even in the parks.

I first realized this on a trip to Rouge Park when my bike and I nearly collided with a homeless man camped in the middle of the Rouge Park Trail.

I've realized this during weekly jogs through the woodlands of Belle Isle, where I've startled more unsuspecting weed smokers than I have squirrels or songbirds or opossums.

I've realized this every time I visit some untamed corner of a Detroit park where I run into someone who utters, just like me, "I'm sure no one ever comes back here."

Don't get me wrong, I'm not complaining. I like to see our parks, our neighborhoods populated. But that doesn't mean that when this "empty" city starts feeling crowded, I don't revel in its loneliest open spaces.

Where I live in Rivertown is both developed and overgrown. It's concrete gray and summer-sprinkler green. In fact, Rivertown boasts more green space than people realize. For starters, there's the RiverWalk, where all of Detroit—black, white, young, old, Hispanic, Middle Eastern—strolls through its concrete plazas. A little farther down, there's the Milikin State Park Wetlands where I've spotted muskrats rustling in the well-manicured brush. There's the Dequindre Cut and the Outdoor Adventure Center and every park from Chene to Mt. Elliot to Gabriel Richard. I've seen all of these places sit empty. I've seen all of them attract a crowd. But with the exception of a few fair weather days, the crowds of Detroit's parks are the kind that let us all still breathe. I'm grateful for that.

That's not to say that Detroit's parks are underutilized. In fact, in Rivertown, I think it's the opposite. Take a summer cruise down our stretch of Jefferson between downtown and the villages, and you'll notice a surprising concentration of active, neon-clad joggers and cyclists enjoying their outdoor recreation options. We may not be as ubiquitous as the joggers of D.C. or the cyclists of Seattle, but Detroiters, in no small number, like to play outside, and Rivertown is our playground. It's something to celebrate.

Of course, the most popular playground attraction is and always has been Belle Isle—the pinnacle of Detroit's great outdoors and first bastion of city solitude. When Frederick Law Olmsted helped design Belle Isle in the eighteenth century, he intended for it to remain as empty as possible. He allowed for the development of some man-made structures—walking paths, sports fields, canals—but he wanted to keep the human touch minimal.

"Openness is the one thing you cannot get in buildings," he once wrote. "What we want to gain is tranquility and rest to the mind."

For the most part, openness isn't hard to find in Detroit. Tranquility can still be found on Belle Isle. But on those rare, beloved summer days, Belle Isle, Detroit, and Rivertown feel full, and that's a good thing. Whenever some out-of-towner makes the inane argument that Detroit is empty, that no one really lives here, I point to Belle Isle in the summer. I point to Rivertown.

But secretly, I relish Detroit's emptiness, because I suspect it won't last forever. I suspect that in the next hundred years, the vacant green spaces of Detroit, populated only by a few neighbors similarly seeking a gulp of fresh air, will no longer be empty.

So for now, in Rivertown, where I'm proud to see the parks half full, I quietly celebrate the empty stretches of the Dequindre Cut. I take joy in the light, early-morning foot traffic of the Riverfront, and I revel in those late off-season evenings, when I am certain I am the last jogger to leave Belle Isle at dusk.

And then I glance behind me, on the bridge I thought was empty, to find someone else reveling in the same solitude.

# West Village: A Five-Year Reflection

*Julién Goodman*

*I*n 2011, I moved to West Village with a group of my friends. We were young twenty-somethings looking for a peaceful homestead on the Eastside—away from all the hubbub of Midtown and Downtown. Then, West Village was still largely an Eastside secret. There was life, yes indeed. It was a beautiful life, a creative life—an original one to say the least. Today, I have people snapping photos of my townhouse and SUVs from Georgia and New York slowly rolling down the streets, with excited passengers pointing out the windows at buildings.

We were kids five years ago, poor kids without trust funds. Of course we were going to have parties. Of course we were going to make our porch light green and plant tomatoes in our front yard and host travelers and just have fun. Of course we were going to make mistakes; that is called life, young life. Our neighbors liked us and put up with our shenanigans. I felt truly welcomed. Back then, I was still greeted on the street by every single person. In the last two years I've had roughly twenty new neighbors move in, most of whom I don't know and have never greeted me. I'd like to not assume things. I am sure they are great people once you get to know them.

Back then the liquor store at the corner of Agnes and Van Dyke was still open, and you could still buy weed from the big man who stood at that corner. And yes, I had friends who did. No harm, happy people. Honestly, I never liked that liquor store. It was dingy and everything in there was stale. If I wanted some whiskey for the house, I usually walked down to the store on Jefferson. Sometimes I'd go to parties and friends of friends would talk about redeveloping that corner; they'd talk about members of the "creative class," which oftentimes meant people who did not current- ly live in the neighborhood. They'd talk about land values and prospective buying and house flipping. And they'd talk about rebuilding their community. They'd talk whatever their fancies or hustles were. I don't blame them; they were and are living their lives and supporting their families. Today, I sit a couple doors down from the old liquor store, sunbathing and sipping coffee from Portland while I attempt to tune out varied conversations of dog training, trips to Amsterdam, and where one buys the best fitted floral shirts.

I am satisfied—wearing a floral shirt myself.

Occupied homes emanated care and love back then as they still do now. Manicured lawns and trimmed shrubs are not a new phenomenon. It is true there were more abandoned homes—some that posed a real threat to the neighborhood. Sometimes they were secured, but oftentimes they were wide open, full of despair and very real reminders of the people who once lived there. I've watched my fair share of homes on fire in Detroit. Keeping them orderly and boarded up was and still is a frequent initiative of local church groups and youth volunteers.

Over three years ago, we had that record-breaking, bone-chilling, polar vortex of a winter. That winter was a fight to stay alive—our pipes burst, our cars were frozen into the street, our heating system was failing, and I specifically remember my boots not being waterproof. You couldn't go outside without the risk of frostbite. And yet, even though it was horribly bitter outside, when someone's car got stuck, people left their homes and helped. That same genuine care came through during neighborhood house fires, robberies, and even dog fights. I experienced it. And I felt it.

My viewpoint here is really not a polarized one, but rather reflective of the rapid change West Village has been experiencing. I love the businesses in my neighborhood. Craft Work is now our neighborhood bar, replacing the old Harlequin Café, which went out of business even before I moved in. And there are a slew of other restaurants and cafés around, with more on the way. Long-time residents are not being left out of the equation either. When Goodness Gracious Alive, a florist on the corner of Van Dyke and Kercheval, moved in, I met Kelley Jones, who is now a friend and business partner. She's been doing arrangements for most of her life; it is something truly special to see her finally have her own storefront—a storefront mentioned in an article in *Model D*. This article, along with Mayor Mike Duggan's notable mention of Kelley during a State of the City Address, seems to imply that Kelley is moving with the waves of "New Detroit"—whatever that means.

I have a lifetime of memories in Detroit and across the country. This illustrative shift of what was then and what is now is a change that must be embraced because, in large, it has already happened—but that doesn't mean we cannot help write what is to come.

# When Ruby Jones Was Here

*Lakisha Dumas*

When Ruby Jones was here, Detroit was where I called home.

Recalling my elementary-school-aged self, bursting through my grandparents' screen door to go outside each day.

That screen door that I could only run out of only a few times before Ruby revoked my outside privileges.

That screen door I am thinking of led to sunny skies, friendly neighbors, fun-filled days, life lessons, and endless possibilities.

That screen door on Algonquin Street led me to becoming a neighborhood-renowned chef at the age of five, in my friend Nicole Belcher's backyard. We would make the fanciest, most spectacular mud pies in the area and if I remember correctly, the tastiest ones, too. I learned with hard work, you could even make dirt beautiful. It is not about what you have but about what you do with what you have.

That same screen door led me to becoming a scholar at six years of age. My front porch is where Louis Jones had class and my grandfather bestowed his wisdom and knowledge to me or whomever, whenever he had the opportunity. I wish I could bottle his wisdom and sell it today. At the time I didn't realize on that front porch, he was giving me his most valuable treasures.

My grandparents' screen door led me to one of my greatest adventures of all time, the time me and my big cousin Nettie took a walk to the penny candy store on Jefferson and Algonquin with all of our friends. Picture it, about eight girls ranging in ages from six to twelve years old, in the middle of the street walking four blocks to one of the busiest streets in Detroit to go to one of the many ultimate penny candy stores in our neighborhood. There appeared to be over 200 types of candy my $2 could buy; I could have gotten one of each. I still remember Gumby playing on the thirteen-inch color television behind the store's counter. I learned during the trip the world was huge and there was so much more to see.

That screen door that was two houses away from Goethe Street led me to becoming a death-defying stunt women at seven years old, when I got on my red Strawberry Shortcake bike and flew for what seemed like at least ten minutes, chin-first into the sidewalk in front of Mr. Price's house. I remember being in the air and thinking to myself, "How is this going to end?" That moment right there, I realized I was much tougher and stronger than I ever imagined.

That gray metal screen door located at 3407 Algonquin Street led to me meeting a legendary superstar when my uncle Louie walked me down the block for me to discover I was about to shake hands with Stevie Wonder, because he was visiting his cousin who lived on their street. My block was so special, Stevie Wonder used to visit. I learned then life was filled with surprises and opportunities. I could be whoever I wanted to be because success was obtainable from right where little old me used to live.

As I close my eyes to reminisce, I instantly feel the warmth today from all the hearts of those who lived on Algonquin Street between Mack Avenue and Goethe Street between 1977 and 1988. My memories give me hope for the city that I once knew so well.

The streetlights were my sign each night my family was about to call my name, and the same anticipation I felt swinging that screen door to the left to the world outside, I felt when swinging it to the right, to the love that lived inside of Ruby's house.

Because when Ruby Jones was here, Detroit was where I called my home.

# Just Off Mack Avenue, on the Detroit Side

*Monica Hogan*

Mack Avenue weaves through my childhood like a thread, like a hem defining the border of my neighborhood on Detroit's far east side, the one the map calls Morningside. If this is a 1960s movie set, then the aerial wide shot opens at the far end of Audubon Road, with a quick glance across Mack, outside the city, to the sparse school playground on the right, then a tight shot on the tall Catholic church on the left, and a pan to the family approaching the traffic stop at the Detroit side, the girls in white gloves and chapel veils, patent leather instead of saddle shoes, because it's time for Sunday Mass.

Mack Avenue cuts through St. Clare's parish as a dividing line. First graders, in dress shirts and ties, uniforms and beanies, learn on the first day of school to queue up in single file on either side of the hallway. We exit left for Charlevoix or right for Mack Avenue, Grosse Pointers on one side, Detroiters on the other, an early if unwitting lesson in us versus them.

In that no-man's land between Mack and Charlevoix, the parochial school building and the church next door connect by way of an underground tunnel, where boys in dark suit coats and girls in pastel dresses line up by height as they approach the stage for the annual spring concert.

The aerial camera frames a wider shot, flying high above St. Clare's steeple and moving past Charlevoix and Kercheval, up to St. Paul and Jefferson Avenue, and scanning Lake St. Clair for sailboats and freighters. The shot retreats again, over the green lawns at Three Mile Park and the mansions with circular driveways, until the mansions turn back to houses, and then the camera crosses Mack Avenue into Detroit and the lens settles over an archway of trees onto a perfectly ordinary residential street.

On that block, the brick 1920s-era houses have four bedrooms, sometimes five, and multiple bathrooms, and that one or two extra bedrooms makes all the difference for families with seven, eight, nine, or ten kids. This is the post-World War II baby boom, after all, and these families are practicing Catholics.

The alleys behind the shops along Mack Avenue snake through the commercial district like a scavenger hunt, treasure troves of empty boxes and stray cats, of discarded beer bottles that fetch two cents a pop, and two cents is real money because penny candy costs a penny at the narrow party store on Mack. It takes a hop, skip, and a jump to get there in bare feet when the tar-paved streets radiate summer heat.

Mack Avenue cuts through my wonder years like a runway, an on-ramp to agency and independence in the days before helicopter parents, in the land of the walkable community. Allowance is handed out in pennies, nickels, and dimes; enough, if saved over time, to buy tiny birthday toys at Joe's Village or a bottle of Brut aftershave for Father's Day from Devonshire Drugs, but not the premium size or there won't be enough left over for a trip to the Kresge's five-and-dime up on Warren or a chocolate milkshake at the Sanders next door—make that two straws, please, so I can share with my little sister.

Mack Avenue shoots through the riots of 1967 like a siren on a fire truck, like a warning, like a threat, like a question: could the troubles we see on the evening news reach all the way to our block, to our house?

Mack Avenue rises through the neighborhood like a spine, a support system for the stay-at-home moms up and down each perpendicular road. Houses are equipped with bread chutes for home delivery and the milk man visits several times a week, but mothers still find cause to send their kids on last-minute errands to the corner store. To garner goodwill, shopkeepers let the locals hang up hand-made posters promoting missing pets or backyard fairs. On our street, the coolest boy on the block offers up forty-fives from his record collection as prizes for the carnival's wheel of fortune.

As the sixties fade into the seventies, Mack Avenue tiptoes through the counterculture, courting flower children and free spirits with colorful beads and candles and incense, with an influx of gift shops named Ole and Kaleidoscope and the Mole Hole, with streetlights dressed up in Tiffany-style lamp shades.

Mack Avenue speeds through the segregated community like a getaway car, like connective tissue to the outside world. A mailbox on the corner takes letters to pen pals in the suburbs and box tops to cereal companies across the country, ones that promise a shiny new prize in exchange for brand loyalty. But the real prize up on Mack is the bus that transports me all the way to Hudson's downtown, to a cosmopolitan center worlds away from mid-century Morningside.

From a distance, a quieter, less trafficked Mack rumbles through my nightmares like an accusation: where did you go? But the house where I grew up with eight siblings, and the street I shared with my best friends, where we played kickball and pinochle and Marco Polo, they still appear in my fondest dreams.

Now, nearly three decades after my parents left Morningside, well after the last of their boomer children left home, Mack Avenue flows through me like a muse, like a ghost, like electricity, zapping me with a small shock of recognition when I pass a namesake Mack truck (never mind that the motor vehicles weren't made in the Motor City at all, and the avenue was named not to honor said vehicles or their creators, not like the Ford Freeway or the Chrysler).

Mack Avenue reverberates through me like a magnetic pulse, pulling my heart back to the east side of Detroit. Pulling me home.

# Alleys

### Michael Constantine McConnell

*A*fter thugs shot my grandfather, Gus, in the neck, Anne Marie and I learned to better distinguish between the firecracker explosions and gunshot thunder that punctuated inner-city Detroit's street music of laughing children, yelling mothers, drunk and raving fathers. Anne Marie, my mother's youngest sister, was seven years old at the time, and I was barely three. My mother and I lived with Anne Marie and their parents, my grandparents—Gus and Mary—in the yellow brick house on the corner of Hazelridge and Peoria in northeast Detroit. By that time in the mid-1970s, the city's industrial heart had all but stopped beating, and our neighborhood remained as a limb that hadn't completely decomposed yet.

Anne Marie and I began our lives at the beginning of the 1970s, well into the collapse of Detroit's automotive prosperity; we grew up in a gray space between two worlds. We lived in a neighborhood of beautiful two-and-three story houses falling into disrepair, proof of the industrial city's decline and evidence of that short distance between prosperity and poverty. Across Peoria, the side street next to the yellow brick house, Anne Marie and I would run in the gravel covered schoolyard of Robinson Elementary School. We played with wildflowers behind the yellow brick house. We threw rocks at garages. In the alley, we played like royalty under lilac blossoms, and when somebody we didn't know walked, stumbled, or crawled toward us, we ran back to the yellow brick house, retreating into one of its many rooms or its cavernous basement.

When we weren't playing in the alley, we'd play in the house's front yard—in the shade of the four tall evergreen trees that Gus and Mary had planted to celebrate the births of their first four children: my mother, Aunt Carolyn, Aunt Marie Anne, and Uncle Tommy. After their last child, Anne Marie, was born, Gus and Mary planted a mulberry tree. Throughout our early childhood, Anne Marie and I smeared our pant-asses across the juice-drenched ground and counted gunshots and firecrackers in the distance. When the sounds came too close, we could run into the yellow brick house to seek protection from Detroit, but nothing could protect us from Mary's Mississippi racism and Gus's alcohol-magnified, Macedonian rage.

"Mary, I'll be home in a little while—after I lose at the table," Gus had called home to say on that night when he got shot. Though he'd always keep this promise, he never came home early. He was an excellent pool player, and the drunker Gus became, the better he played. Usually, long after last call, the bartender would make him stop and turn him out into the cold Detroit morning.

On that night, Gus probably stumbled over the curb and into the same wet, cold street where he'd lain two years earlier with a bruised face and broken back after a similar night of winning at pool. He probably walked down an alley and passed the same dumpster he'd leaned against on another night with a knife wedged into his stomach near his rotting liver. Intending to bring home a platter of baklava for his family, who would wake up soon, Gus might have been walking to a nearby Greek store owned by another barfly, a friend who might be awake still.

"Hey, you sons of bitches," Gus undoubtedly snarled at the group of young black men, punctuating his words with obscene thumb gestures like drunk old Macedonian men do.

If the bullet had been a centimeter closer to his jugular vein, doctors told Gus when he woke up in a hospital with a hangover and a patched hole near his throat, he surely would have died. So he stayed away from the bars for a while and sat at home, smoking cigarettes and tinkering with broken vacuum cleaners and industrial buffing machines that he would eventually try to resell. He'd whine and complain about his toothaches and hemorrhoids, about the economic slump, about how ten years earlier he made more money in a half-day of work than he could now in a week. And he'd make lists. As the long black strands of his greased hair hung like curved pincers over his face and yellow smoke rolled through his nostrils, he'd make lists of people he hated.

"That son of a bitch Jablonski is number two on the list this week, Mary," he'd yell to my grandmother in the kitchen, who would be conjuring headcheese out of boiled pig snouts and knuckles, a Baltic recipe called "piftea" that she'd learned from her mother-in-law.

"I wouldn't piss on that Malaka if he was on fire," Gus would say, then stand, walk across the living room, and spit out the front door. After hacking coughs shook his body, he'd palm the hole in his neck and yell, "Oh, Jesus Christ!"

One time, I asked, "Dad, what's a Malaka?" I called him Dad because that's what my mother and aunts and Anne Marie called him. I didn't know my biological father, so Gus was the only person I knew by that name.

"Go ask your grandmother," he said, dismissing me. I walked into the kitchen to ask my grandmother, who hovered over her cauldron and talked to women drinking coffee at the breakfast table.

"I've said it before, and I mean it. If any one of my kids marries an A-rab, Mexican, or Colored, I'll disown them, and I won't recognize their children as my grandchildren," she said to the other women. Thinking of the little Asian girl down the alley who Anne Marie and I played with, I asked from ground level, "What about Chinese girls, Baba?"

"Yeah," she exclaimed, snubbing her cigarette butt into a tin tray and shaking a new one from her pack. "None of them Chinks, either!" At such a young age, I did not understand my grandmother's racism. Born and raised in Pott's Camp, Mississippi, she'd brought along her Old South hatred when her father moved the family up north to Detroit so he could work at Ford. Whereas my grandmother would talk about "Niggers and Chinks," I was still innocent enough to accept a person simply as a person, and a child—as I was—simply as a child.

"Baba, what's a Malaka?" I asked her.

"Dammit, Gus," she said under her breath, trying not to smile. "Go ask your grandfather, Michael. He'll tell you. Now go, or I'm going to cut off your ding and put it in the piftea. Go play with Anne Marie." She pointed her gangly yellow finger toward the living room and stared at me with eyes that could cast shadows on hell's floor. As I scrambled out of the kitchen, she braced a hand against her waist, threw her head back, and exhaled cigarette smoke that, like her laughter, settled into every corner of the enormous house.

When Anne Marie and I walked down the alley behind the yellow brick house, we could see other children playing, people working on cars in their yards, mothers and grandmothers hanging diapers across a clothesline to dry, the older kids shooting rats with BB guns. When a rat would get hit, we could hear the shrill cry and see it jump above the tall grass toward the sky, then land running. My grandmother would periodically leave the kitchen and the piftea and check the alley to see if we were there.

"I better not catch you two in the alley again, or you'll both get whooped," she would say. She would always talk about how the neighborhoods were once beautiful and calm, but that after the riots in the sixties—the riots that scarred the city by burning neighborhoods into charred fields that remained undeveloped because the property value was so low, because the murder rate was so high—the city just hadn't been safe. But we'd play in the alley anyway. We'd play and fight in the weeds that grew from dirt lines along the house, where the pale yellow walls of 14200 Hazelridge entered deep earth. We'd play with all of the other inner-city children who lived along the same alley and had escaped to there briefly.

The yellow brick house anchored a street corner, so there was a side street on one side and nine houses on the other. Most of Detroit's streets were set up with ten houses making one city block. Ten city blocks approximated a mile, and the main streets running east and west had corresponding numerical names, like Six Mile Road and Seven Mile Road. Most of the roads ran east-west or north-south with a few streets running diagonally, intercepting all other streets. As a French fort, Detroit had burned to the ground, ignited by an airborne pipe ember. The survivors adopted a plan to rebuild the fort into a city that loosely resembled wheel-spokes spreading from the downtown area near the shore of the Detroit River, forming a broad half-moon. Expansion and development naturally occurred geometrically, segmenting the entire city into a sea of squares and rectangles. For trash removal, alleyways cut like empty spines through every city block, creating an alternating pattern of ten houses, alley, ten houses, street, ten houses, alley, ten houses, street, and so on.

Anne Marie and I played in the alley one day when Gus stumbled home from the bar on an early Sunday afternoon about two months after he'd been shot. He had just started drinking again, but for those two months there'd been no screaming arguments, no violence, no reasons to hide.

"Hey, you kids get out of that alley right now," he yelled to us, the words sliding loosely from his mouth. He pressed both hands against the right side of his face and stumbled to the front porch. We ran through the back door of the yellow brick house, through the kitchen, and into the living room, where Gus swayed in the middle of the floor, next to my grandmother.

"Oh, Jesus Christ, Mary," he said through clenched teeth, hissing his J's and S's. "If that son of a bitch dentist can do it, so can I. Just get me the goddamned pliers." Then he was still, and he looked at his wife in the scary way that usually made me and Anne Marie run, but he hadn't raised his hand to her; he didn't wield a wrench or crowbar, so we didn't run. We could tell Gus was in pain, and Mary hurried to get the pliers, anxious to dare him.

"Dad," asked Anne Marie. "Are you alright?"

"Oh, yeah, sweetie," he said, holding his jaw and short-hopping up and down. "I'll be all right." With my fingers in my mouth, I watched my grandfather as if I were watching a movie or cartoon and waiting to see what the main character would do next.

"Here you go, doctor," my grandmother said, pushing a silver pair of pliers at him. After he snatched the tool from her, she crossed her arms and stood there with a cigarette between her lips, watching attentively as her husband worked the pliers around the sore tooth in his open mouth. Even the birds in the trees outside of the yellow brick house were still for that space in time when Gus paused with pliers under his lip, and only stained-glass-filtered light from the sunroom windows dared to move, flooding the room with color and resting wraith diamonds on the carpet behind his knees. Gus's tooth twisting away from the pulpy roots under his gums sounded like a candy cane being slowly twisted in half.

"Oh my God," said Mary, and she walked away.

"We gotta put it in water, Dad," said Anne Marie, and she ran to the kitchen.

I was young, barely past diapers. I didn't know what to think as my primary male role model defined my worst fear and acted it out in front of my eyes. He showed me how to supplement loss of control with misplaced aggression. I stood still and watched, with my fingers in my mouth. Gus wailed deep and arched his body backward, clutching his mouth, then he bent forward and spit blood into his hands.

Anne Marie returned with a jar full of water, grabbed the tooth from the ground, and dropped it into the jar. Shades of pink from the bloody tooth washed through the water as it fell into the bottom with that sterile click of glass tapping against bone. Gus clung to the carpet and moaned. Anne Marie held the jar above her head, inspecting the tooth at all angles as if it were an unwrapped toy on Christmas morning. I returned to the alley and sat down on the ground, arranging rocks into square patterns, like I was building my own little city of city blocks, and mile roads, and alleys. Across the side street stood the elementary school I'd start the next fall. After that would be suicides. After that would be cancers. Before long, as usual, my grandmother came to get me.

"C'mon Michael, time for dinner; the piftea's ready." I tried again to ask her what a Malaka was, but she cut me off by telling me things she would tell me when she caught me playing in the alley. She told me that the alley is a place where gangs hide and hang out, where roving bands of dogs scavenge for food. Where people sleep. Where bodies are found.

# War Hero

## *Hakeem Weatherspoon*

Boom boom
Bang bang
Let the sirens sang.

What's the town that my people say?

We are in cities, let my people pray!

We call it rising from the ashes,

They call it dying, to not live today.

They continue to Scream,

Let them die let them die!

I'm a war prisoner with a dream,
that one day, once more, the sun will shine on the darkside once more.

I believe that anything is possible and anything can be conquered.

Where I'm from,
You're chained to a generational institutional school of thought
That's keeping you ignorant, but yet not bliss.

Not having a lump sum of knowledge opens the battlefield
Of Rhetorical war.

Fighting, everyday to make ends meet.

Fighting, everyday to put food on the table.

Fighting, everyday to live for the free.

Fighting, everyday to have home for the brave.

Fighting, and still fighting,

For,
An American Dream.

Life isn't easy where I'm from.

I cry,
Allow me to speak,
For my people,
To speak to you people, to a degree
That hell's fire couldn't burn.

I hope that you'll learn,
That every war has two heroes.

As my heart beats
With warmth, and melts the cold hearts of the people.
I am my people's hero!
I am the oxygen, when their sky is the limit and it has fallen down to their
height and crushed them as if there wasn't no Tomorrow.
Even though their today is not their tomorrow,
I sorrow,
For Hope.

The opposing side see their hero as if this war is not only hurting one side
It's hurting today's tomorrow.

It's hurting the youth to the wise of a great future.

So, every side has a hero when the battle is over.
One will die for their side.
One will live to bring their side a better tomorrow.

# Poletown

## Drew Philp

*9* was running an errand on Forestdale on my day off to work on my house. It was sunny and warm, and I was feeling rather okay. I probably needed to borrow a tool from Paul or Molly or someone, but I wasn't in too big of a hurry to get back to the dark of my house and get filthy, charging some project.

Paul or anyone else didn't seem to be around. I walked down the street, knocking on a few doors, and couldn't get anyone. A man I had never met, obviously from the neighborhood, rode down the street on a bike. He stopped.

"Hey!"

I didn't answer to "hey" any longer and paid him no mind and continued on my way. He called again.

"Hey! Hey mister." I stopped this time.

I gave him a good look over. He was old enough to be my father and rotund. He had a short, neat beard and a diamond stud in one ear. His bike was well cared for. I liked his face. It wasn't mean or hard, and his eyes were clear, not jaundiced from too much to drink or bloodshot with drugs.

"What do you need, bud?"

"Do you know that farmer who lives around here? He used to run horses around. Real funny guy. A white guy."

"Yeah, but he's not home right now. What do you need to talk to him about?"

"Oh I ain't selling nothing. I'm not selling nothing." He waved his hand about his chest. "Listen man, I got a problem—"

"Don't we all."

"I got this baby raccoon. He's about this big." He held his fingers in a circle about the size of a dinner roll. "I saved him. Him and his brother. Some kids down the way killed his mother, they was beating him, and they were about to get him too but I chased 'em away. His brother died right there in my hands. I got him a little cage and I've been feeding him applesauce in a jar top, like off a pickle jar." He held his hands up in a circle again to show me the size of the jar top. "I called the animal doctor down there downtown and that's what they told me to feed 'em. My wife is making me get rid of him and I don't want to just let him go. He ain't big enough yet to make it out there." He gestured toward the neighborhood. "I just wanted to see if that farmer might take him."

"I don't know if Paul's going to want a raccoon."

"You have to help me. You gotta help me, man. I can't just turn him out. He'll die." I could see that he meant it. Whatever he had, he cared for it.

"Maybe Molly can take it. I'll go see."

She had built a room in her house for a pair of baby pheasants, rescued when their mother was killed by a car. She might not be able to say no. I knocked on her door; no answer.

"She ain't home either man. I'm sorry, brother. I don't know what else to tell you."

"Will you take me down to Belle Isle, to that nature zoo they have? They might want it."

"Can't you drive?"

"I don't got no car man," he went into something about the VA hospital downtown, and some checks and whatnot.

"I don't think they're going to want a raccoon either. I don't think they take that kind of thing."

"Please."

I looked around for some kind of escape. There was no one else around.

"Alright. I'll meet you back here in fifteen minutes."

"Thanks man, thank you." He smiled for the first time and sped off on his bike.

Sure enough, in fifteen minutes he was back with the cage. There was a tiny raccoon stuffed inside with his back in the corner, his claws out, and his fangs bared. There was a water bottle, the kind you water hamsters with, a blanket, and a jar lid of applesauce.

"Hey little guy," I put my finger close to the cage to pet him and he gnashed his teeth. "Woah. He sure is alive, ain't he?" He would have been cute as an internet cat if he wasn't so frightened and jostled from the bike ride over. The man cooed and talked to it like it was a baby.

I knew you could turn raccoons into pets if you got them at this age. My godmother was from the dirt-floor hollers of Kentucky, and her parents had a raccoon for a pet. It was obese and would waddle around the house and climb up in your lap and turn its belly upside down to be pet. I used to play with it when I was a kid, roll around with it on the floor, sleep with it even. They're like a cross between a dog and a cat, more friendly than feline, less blindly loyal than canine.

"You sure you don't want to keep this little guy?"

"My wife said she wouldn't have it in the house one more day. It's gotta go."

We drove to Belle Isle with the raccoon screaming in the back of the truck as we exchanged niceties.

When we got to the zoo, I wandered around and looked at the spiders and lizards and things they had in tanks while Jimmy talked to the lady at the desk. They didn't want it either. After some more haggling, the woman suggested he could leave it in the forest behind the zoo.

"You think he'll make it back there?" he said so earnestly the woman's composure almost broke. "He's just tiny." He held up the cage for good measure and the coon hissed.

"Oh, he'll be fine. Just fine." She shot me a skeptical look and I went back to the frogs.

"Do you think another veterinarian will want him?" He had already tried one. He tried the pound too but they didn't take wild animals.

"I think it'll be best if you just leave him out back there." The woman got out from behind her desk and placed her arm around Jimmy, leading him toward the door. "He's going to be just fine." She looked at me again. It was time to go.

"Are you coming too?" he asked the woman.

"No, I have to stay here at the desk. I'm sure your friend will help you."

The mosquitos were ragged in the woods behind the zoo. I guess the canopy made it cool enough for them during the day. We walked in about a hundred yards before I told Jimmy this was where we're going to leave him.

"So what do we do?" Jimmy asked me.

"What do you mean?"

"How do we get him out of here?"

"Just open the cage and leave it on the ground. Get that applesauce and put it in front of the door. He'll come out to get it."

He set the cage down and opened the door.

"Can we say a prayer?" Jimmy asked, and looked up at me. His eyes were beginning to water. This grown man I'd just met was about to cry in front of me. We both bowed our heads. After an appropriate time I said, "Well, we got to get him out of there somehow."

Jimmy looked up. "I thought you were going to say a prayer."

"Oh, ah, I don't really know any prayers."

"Just say something, anything." The raccoon hadn't moved from its spot in the back of the cage, his little black eyes wild and his teeth white.

"Ah, okay. We are gathered here to say goodbye to, to, what's his name?"

"Rocco."

"To Rocco the raccoon. He was a good raccoon, but he has to go back into the wild on Belle Isle from whence he came. I'm sure he will love it and be happy forever. Amen."

"Amen."

"Jimmy, we have to get him out of there somehow. He's not coming and I can't wait any longer. I have to get back to work."

"Well, then what should we do?"

"Get a stick and poke him out."

"I don't want to hurt him."

"He'll be fine."

After some rumbling and scratching and hissing, he was gone into the underbrush.

"Come on Jimmy." The guy was headed towards the bush with his arms out. "Come on Jimmy." I put my arm around him and led him back to the truck. We sat down and I closed my door.

"Do you think he's going to make it?" Jimmy asked me, tears streaming down his cheeks.

# A One-Year Stand in Hamtramck

*Aaron Foley*

There is Highland Park, and there is Hamtramck. For many of us that grow up in Detroit, you typically know one very well, and barely the other. But here's what little I knew about Hamtramck in the beginning: my great-grandmother, Ruth, lived in the projects on Charles Street on the Detroit side of Hamtramck. My other great-grandmother, California, died at her family home on Arlington Street, which dead-ends in Hamtramck. California's daughter, my grandmother, shopped in Hamtramck for formal wear back in the day. For years, my relatives had tangential connections to the mostly Polish, working-class, factory town inside the border of Detroit, but we were culturally more in tune with Highland Park, where some of us actually lived.

Sometime in the 1990s, my cousin, one of California's granddaughters, bought a home in Hamtramck. Her mother, my great-aunt, still lived on Arlington, and Hamtramck was a fine alternative to being on the east side of Detroit without *being* on the east side of Detroit, if you get what I mean. By that time, abandonment and economic strife had already started settling in nicely in parts of the east side (west side, too)—Arlington Street was not immune. Somehow, even though Dodge Main closed years ago, Hamtramck survived.

Still, I had only a distant connection to this little town growing up. It was an oddity that I only knew for my cousin's house, a sausage factory, and a place where people went for Fat Tuesday. I do remember, however, going shopping with my grandmother for the aforementioned formal wear, and us stopping at a music shop so I could buy Usher's "U Make Me Wanna" on a cassette single—and I didn't know then that it would become, as the media would describe, Michigan's most international city, with nearly every country in the world represented. Poland, yes, but also almost every other eastern European country, and a few from the Middle East and

South Asia as well.

A few years ago I wrote a book called *How to Live in Detroit Without Being a Jackass*, and sometime between the contract to publish and when the book hit shelves, my relationship with my partner deteriorated. The story of how *that* happened may be for another book. But along the way, I had a backup plan that (unfortunately) came to fruition: moving to Hamtramck. A few times while my ex and I were renovating our west side Detroit house, I'd venture into Hamtramck to check things out. By this time in the mid-2010s, Hamtramck was not only home to fourth- and fifth-generation Poles and Ukrainians—and the Bangladeshis, Yemenis, and Indians that followed—but also to, of coure, twenty-something hipsters in search of the cheap housing that was quickly becoming out of reach in certain parts of Detroit. And when I say "certain parts," I mean the parts of Detroit that are within relative distance of downtown but still dense of enough to have arts and entertainment.

After my ex and I had the big blowup, I packed up my belongings and temporarily moved to mom's house. And despite my persona as Mr. Detroit—that's what one of my best friends called me—I felt the call to Hamtramck getting louder. I looked at apartments in Palmer Park, I tried to find something cheap in Midtown, Woodbridge's Facebook group scared the hell out of me, and although I loved Southwest Detroit, I wasn't as intricately familiar with it like I was with the east side or west side.

But Hamtramck checked all the boxes. It was hella convenient, as I-75 cut right through town and both I-94 and the Davison were not too far away. Holbrook was just a mile or so from Woodward Avenue, and Grand Boulevard was at the southern edge of town. It offered all the walkability of say, a Birmingham or a Royal Oak, but wasn't as blindingly glossy as the former, nor did it have the chain takeover of the latter. A few acquaintances had moved here in recent years and had no complaints. And above all, it was cheap as fuck. "I'm only going to stay here for a little bit," I told myself. Get in, get out. Pay cheap rent, save your money, and go right back to Detroit.

Eventually, I did go back to Detroit. But the temptation to stay in Hamtown was pretty strong.

I remember one of the first places I looked at—the price was a very affordable $550 a month, but not only was it in desperate need of renovation, a roach scurried across the kitchen floor during my viewing. *"Shit, no wonder it's so cheap,"* I thought. The other challenge was finding something pet-friendly. I was warned that because a significant number of landlords in Hamtramck come from countries that frown upon pets, it was always awkward when I mentioned that I had a one-hundred-pound German Shepherd mix that would also occupy the residence.

With patience, I found a two-bedroom, single-family place on Lumpkin Street, one of the bigger, more recognizable streets in town. A single-family home was already hard to come by in Hamtramck; the vast majority of rentals are in flats and buildings. And the price—$600 a month, plus an extra $25 for the dog—was a steal, at least according to other residents. There's a part of me that will never pay above a certain threshold for rent in Detroit proper, and certainly the same applied to Hamtramck. I lucked out, and by the Fourth of July that year, I was Hamtramck's newest arrival.

Up the street from my little white bungalow was Caniff Avenue, one of the town's main arteries. I was one block away from Carpenter Avenue, which separated part of Hamtramck's northwestern border from east side Detroit. And I was around the corner from on-ramps to I-75. It was all so convenient, but I had to keep reminding myself, "Get in, get out. Don't get attached."

My first week there was hell. Besides DTE Energy taking its sweet time to turn the gas back on (which meant a week of cold showers), I got a speeding ticket a few days after moving in, cruising a little too fast in an infamous speed trap along the Hamtramck-Detroit border. Along the I-75 service drive, the speed limit moves from thirty-five miles per hour (Detroit side) to twenty-five miles per hour (Hamtramck side) and back to thirty-five miles per hour (Detroit again), and God help you if you are caught doing thrity-five in the twenty-tive. It was at my court date that I first found out how small and homey Hamtramck is; the presiding judge, a substitute that day, is one of the town's leading lawyers, and her family has been practicing law in Hamtramck for decades. She was understanding enough and didn't give me any points on my license or a hefty fine, but just a warning: this is Hamtramck.

"Get in, get out."

I told very few people I lived in Hamtramck. A few local writers who actually lived in town knew, but there was no Facebook announcement, no Instagram snapshot of the new place. I dropped a few hints here and there, but nothing that expressly said, "Yes, Mr. Detroit actually lives in Hamtramck." After all, we'd reached a point in Detroit—and yeah, I've added fuel to this fire—that unless you actually live in Detroit, you can't say you're from Detroit.

Not even my co-workers at the time knew. I might have told one, who was a drummer for a band that had been featured in the *New York Times* and was touring clubs all over the country. True to Hamtramck form, he was actually one of many musicians—and writers, and artists, and photographers—that lived there. Or maybe I didn't tell him. I recall overhearing a conversation where he and a few others described Hamtramck as being "just like Southwest Detroit." The Detroiter in me wanted to yell, but I wasn't a true Detroiter in that moment.

Since I told almost no one that I lived here, I felt a strange sense of anonymity. In the first few weeks after the speeding ticket, I spent a lot of time walking around town. Hamtramck is only two square miles—smaller than my college campus. My neighborhood was mostly flats, but there were a few small houses with big porches and tall, first-floor windows that almost reminded me of New Orleans. I heard one writer say he lived in the "Grosse Pointe of Hamtramck," so I would walk around, trying to figure out which street that was. Was it Gallagher Street between Carpenter and Casmere, a row of well-kept, 1930s brick houses that could be picked up and dropped off in the Russell Woods neighborhood I grew up in? Or was it the neighborhood surrounding St. Florian Roman Catholic Church, one of the many Catholic churches in town whose bells peal a charming chorus for their neighbors?

There was no neighborhood that felt more or less Grosse Pointe, because while the GPs are well-stocked with wealthy WASPs, Hamtramck most certainly is not.

Oh, that's not to say there isn't some overlap in worldview between older Poles and some of Grosse Pointe's finest, both of whom can be found on online forums borderline furious about the increasing diversity of their respective hometowns. But Hamtramck is a true melting pot on the front burner on the stove that is America.

When you walk around Hamtramck, you hear a lot of rap banging from cars. The thing is, you never know who's driving. Look up, and you might see a black dude with Future turned up, or a Middle Eastern guy bumping something in Arabic—or in English. I won't say rap is Metro Detroit's great unifier. I will say that growing up in a city where the tension between blacks and Arabs was always thick, I was caught off guard each time I heard English-language hip-hop from an Arab man's car. (I also heard Arab teens using "nigga" in casual conversation a few times, but you can't fight all battles.) When you walk along Joseph Campau, Hamtramck's Woodward Avenue, you might hear indie rock coming from a former nail salon that had been converted into a makeshift concert venue. I'd go there when I could—I'm not sure if the place ever had a name beyond the "Q Nails" written on the awning—and drink cheap beer. If you walk along Conant Avenue, you won't see as many blacks, Poles, Catholics, hipster drummers, or Arab rappers, but plenty of Indians and Bangladeshis—beautiful women of all ages in saris and bindis, like a city scene from the Bollywood movies my grandmother was so fond of. When I walked my dog around the neighborhood, sometimes I'd smell familiar Southern recipes, and sometimes it'd be biryani, but all of downtown smelled like Polish sausage.

"I could live here," I found myself saying. But I had to remind myself to get in and get out.

Pretty soon I was knee-deep in the Hamtramck lifestyle, if there is such a thing. I'd been warned that some of the bars in town were "only for Hamtramck regulars," which might have been code for the first wave of aging hipsters frustrated with new folks like me moving in, the old Poles, or maybe both. Instead, I'd belly up at Bumbo's, which, like me, was new in town—a craft-cocktail place that took up residence in one of the older dives. (A much-touted fact is that Hamtramck, at one point, had more bars per capita than any American city.) I'd find myself at Whiskey in the Jar, too. Once, after more than a few drinks there, I woke up with the Hamtramck city clerk's business card in my pocket. There's that small-town thing again, the fact that at some point during a night of drinking at a divey whiskey bar, I'd been in conversation with the town's city clerk. (Apparently everyone in Hamtramck city government has a second job; the mayor owns a vintage clothing store on Joseph Campau.)

I grocery-shopped at Al-Haramain, got doughnuts at Detroit Donut, took a friend to see improv at Planet Ant Theatre, went on a date at Yemen Café, made late-night runs to Steve's Party Store (which just might have the best craft-beer selection in Southeast Michigan despite its workaday exterior), tried (and failed) to incorporate yogurt drinks into my diet, ate too much fried food way too late at night at Campau Tower, and listened to country music at the Painted Lady. That Hamtramck had its own newspaper, the *Hamtramck Observer*, spoke to the journalist in me, but hearing gossip from chatty residents on every corner kept me in tune, too.

I became a quiet observer of the folks in the neighborhood. There was the guy that got stinking drunk on multiple mornings. One time, he fell off some concrete steps and scraped his face in front of kids walking to school. There was the older black woman on the block who knew everybody in town: the mayor, the cops, the librarians, the city council people, everybody. The young lesbian couple down the street with a pit bull they got after a string of break-ins in the neighborhood just before I got there. The big family in a little house who spoke one of the Eastern European languages—I didn't want to ask, but I thought it was cute that even the younger generations spoke it freely, unabashedly. The old black man and his old white male neighbor that took several laps around one of the blocks every morning, talking about the day's news and other happenings.

I suddenly found myself telling a few more people I lived in Hamtramck, and trying to convince everyone to get on board. "Get here while it's still cheap," I'd say. It did seem like a few Facebook friends were asking more and more about Hamtramck, in the context of Midtown getting too pricey. I was starting to feel like the last wave of people in on Hamtramck's secret, and was starting to feel a little prideful. But I'd remind myself to get in, and get out. Don't get attached.

Hamtramck usually gets only media attention around Paczki Day—Fat Tuesday for the rest of the world— when paczki, a Polish pastry that is similar to a doughnut (don't call it a doughnut, please), is served to the masses. A few months after I moved in, however, Hamtramck was on display to the world. The city had elected a new city council, the majority of which practiced Islam. It made Hamtramck the only city in America with a majority-Muslim city council, which meant journalists swarmed the two-square-mile town, wondering if white folks were ready for the change.

The reaction was a collective "meh" from townies. As long as they're not corrupt like those Detroit city council folks, pretty much everyone was cool with it. Hamtramck had already gotten used to mosques, and the Muslim call to prayer played on speakers throughout town. No, there was not going to be sharia law or subtle ordinance changes. No, no one was concerned about any terrorist attacks (there hadn't been any to date, had there?). And sure enough, life went on.

Winter was fairly uneventful, but by spring I was ready to move. Aside from the fact that my landlord was a cheap-ass and refused to call a certified plumber to deal with the basement drain that kept backing up with sewage (few experiences are as humbling as having to literally clean up your own shit, repeatedly) or a certified roofer to deal with the leaks in the living room, it was time to start house-hunting in Detroit. (Plus, *Jackass* was taking off, and there was nothing more awkward than the two-handed explanation of your relationship hitting the skids and the fact that you no longer live in the city you wrote a whole book about.) I set a timeline to be out by July, when my lease was up.

But I'm not gonna lie: I considered a few listings in Hamtramck, even broaching the idea with my landlord about buying the house I was renting and fixing it up myself. Part of me wanted to give Hamtramck a chance. In the year I lived there, there were also a few articles highlighting all the affordability, the diversity, the food, and so on, and more people were catching on. One of those artists' compounds-museums around the corner from me was getting attention (and, by the way, there are quite a few galleries in town), and a floral artist had filled an abandoned house a few blocks away with stunning flower displays. I wagered with coping with FOMO once I left Hamtramck and the longing to be back in a city that's facing its own identity changes.

I settled in a small condo on Detroit's riverfront, where I am now. I got out of Hamtramck at the end of July. But not before taking a few more walks around town.

Around the Fourth of July—before the holiday, but not the day of, I remember —there was a family setting off fireworks in their backyard. Fireworks are annoying in the state of Michigan now since our governor lifted restrictions on bigger, flashier, and deadlier explosives, but these were on a smaller scale, thankfully. From the sidewalk, I watched a trio of women in niqabs in their driveway looking up at the lights in the sky while a man set off each explosive. I remember saying, "Damn, I guess everyone likes fireworks." But Hamtramck was where this was. And I tried not to get attached again.

*Interlude*

# Be Safe

*Justin Rogers*

Safety is only wished
upon those In danger,
like Paris,
like Brussels,
like all the battlegrounds we plant prayers on
before our own then wonder
why our children die
why our roots die
even though we tell them to be safe
whenever they leave our homes.
Safety doesn't grow on our tongues,
is only an infected piercing
handed down to our children.

The last time someone told me to be safe
it stung all the way to my destination—
there was no gospel chord to soothe the paranoia
no trunt trap music amen amen
to protect the ghetto my car becomes
whenever my melanin moves in.

What is safety when you are the definition of danger?
The first time i forgot
to tell someone to be safe
the silence became a luxury
& what is it to own a luxury
if you're watching it leave your home for a casket?
What is the casket but a way
to apologize for
not being safe enough
to curve the bullet
to feed your family
to walk outside.

What is outside but a maze
filled with niggas
an army around the edges?

What are edges except
a street separating wealth & ghetto;
last time I crossed
the armed blue eyes frowned segregation
into my nappy hair & I returned home
grateful for the warning
grateful for the empty houses
& niggas hoodie up
in the street all night
would guarantee upon my arrival?
What safer place is there than habitat?
What safer place is there
than where at least I know
who wants me dead?
What is safer than danger?
What is safer than being black?

The last time I felt safe,
I could easily name someone who did not–
& that is my bigger fear:

That I'll discover safe & forget
the names of everyone still searching

& someone will say
        *That nigga not dangerous*
        *That nigga not black*
        *That nigga just safe—*

Till they come through
with a belly full of
bullets, jail sentences, kinky hair, & hoodies
to remind this nigga
where he came from.

# Highland Park: Stories within Stories in a City within a City

*Bailey Sisoy Isgro*

When people talk about Highland Park, it often sounds like they're remembering their grandmothers; "she was beautiful and vivacious in her day," or "you should have seen her factories humming during the war," or "she was the envy of every man." Trope after trope, anecdote after anecdote, to describe a city within a city. A nearly three-square-mile plot of hallowed industrial ground, completely surrounded by the city of Detroit. A city where the Ford family cemented the $5 a day wage. A city often confused with a neighborhood, where gangsters ran booze, notorious brothels operated, factories revolutionized the employment of women, schools were considered the finest in the nation, and FDR's arsenal of democracy flourished. Indeed it was Highland Park, with its wide, pedestrian-friendly streets and glorious public amenities that became the envy of suburban America. Wealthy, beautiful, and within Detroit, the city of Highland Park flourished, reaching a crescendo at the turn of the nineteenth century, when it was widely considered the finest city in America in which to raise a family.

Yet Highland Park is still here, often passed through without notice in the transition between Detroit's city line and the fashionable suburb of Ferndale. Driving up Woodward Avenue with the Detroit River at your back, you'll spend nearly four minutes in Highland Park—if you manage to catch all four of our traffic lights. Then you'll be back in Detroit for another two miles, past Palmer Park and Woodlawn Cemetery, and out across Eight Mile Road into Ferndale. Cartographically speaking, Highland Park reaches from McNichols in the north to Tuxedo and Tennyson Streets to the south, and the railroad tracks of the Grand Trunk Western Railway Line in the east to the Lodge Freeway in the west. Looking at a map of Detroit, Highland Park—along with its sister enclave, Hamtramck—comprise the gap in the center of any map of Detroit; the hole of the "Detroit doughnut." Even with nearly 12,000 souls calling it home, it's now far smaller by population than back in the glory days, and is in some ways perceived as smaller now than in the pre-automotive era, which is where the story of the city within a city starts.

In those days, Highland Park had yet to be anything other than a handful of family farms, a horse track, a shoe factory, and a health spa and resort of dubious utility. It was a suburb claimed from Michigan wilderness, a wilderness that was more home to bears, turkeys, rabbits, pheasants, beavers, and wolves. Even before that, the swampy swath of land had a history 7,000 years older than its European settlers; it was home to Native Americans, and the hunting and fishing grounds of generations. At the founding of Detroit by the French explorer Cadillac, it was little more than a wetland, rich with trapping and hunting opportunities, and timbers. Throughout the eighteenth and nineteenth centuries, the area was dense and muddy, trekked and explored by early farming families who hedged their ribbon farms against the pools, plowing the rich floodplain soil. Long the ancestral home of Ottawa, Algonquin, and Miami Native Americans, these earliest farming families lived in—and out—of peace in what was undeniably the hostile wilds of the new world.

In the aftermath of the great fire of Detroit in 1805, the federal government granted permission for state officials to sell publicly owned land in order to raise the required funds to rebuild the devastated city. In 1818, Augustus B. Woodward, for whom Woodward Avenue is named, eagerly bought the land, at the time nearly six miles north from the flourishing Detroit city center. By 1825, Woodward had a prominent career as a judge and city official. If history has taught us anything, it is that men who build great big things love to name those things after themselves, and the good judge was no exception; he established the town of Woodwardville on the ridge north of Detroit, with the aptly named Woodward Avenue cutting through it. Although the road was originally called Court House Avenue, the Judge renamed it after himself in the years following the fire of 1805. Woodward, who was known for his self-deprecating humor and false modesty, claimed the road's name was in reference to the fact that it traveled from the wooded area of current day Highland Park to the river; he said that it was "towards the woods" or "wood-ward." (If you believe that, then I have a swamp to sell you.)

Whatever his naming convention, his stint as city planner was far less rewarded than his judicial career, and by 1836 the land had been sold to another judge. Benjamin F. H. Witherell attempted his own village, also on the swamp; he named the village Cassandra, but it too rather quickly failed. As Detroit grew in both physical size and population, the area on the ridge snuck ever closer to prosperity. Mile by mile, its proximity to the great "Paris of the Midwest" shortened until in 1860, just a year before the start of the American Civil War, the twice-failed settlement was granted a United States Post Office and incorporated as the village of Whitewood. The community would send roughly 40 percent of its populace to fight in that war, and the post office closed and reopened no less than four times in the following thirty years, citing lack of use and a small population. However, a strong core of original families had begun to form, and the farming was plentiful.

In 1889, twenty-four years after the Civil War, with Detroit booming and over-flowing with manufacturing spurred on by the industrial revolution, shipping, and train transport, along with an eager workforce of new immigrants, freed slaves, and generational families, the settlement was finally incorporated under the name of Highland Park. The charge was led by the quirky Captain William H. Stevens. A wealthy real estate developer with one eye who'd made a fortune in silver mining, he was an ardent promoter of Highland Park, and stood at the vanguard of citizens rallying to incorporate and thus fend off annexation by Detroit. The native New Yorker dominated the city politically and civically, planning and developing its first extensive waterworks system, building the first school (along with hiring teachers), rallying support for the streetcar system's inclusion of Highland Park, and working with Senator Palmer to create Detroit's Palmer Park. His resort and racetrack attract-ed wealthy Detroiters "up" to Highland Park on weekends, which furthered exposure and economic growth. Upon the death of Captain Stevens in 1901, his legacy in the city only grew. Katherine Whitney McGregor, the daugher of his friend, David Whitney, of the famous Whitney mansion which now stands sentinel as an elegant restaurant on Woodward, bought his home and turned it into the Highland Park home for crippled and homeless children.

Steady but undramatic growth followed as Highland Park found its legs and took its first tentative steps as a desirable Detroit border town. As a small town of 425 people, the most exciting things a Highland Parker might experience were riding a bike up Woodward Ave three miles to an outpost station of the streetcar line, in order to take the streetcar ride into the bustling city center of Detroit; perhaps to the still-present Eastern Market, to sell their farm's wares, or to show a prized animal. Picnickers and the well-to-do of Highland Park could travel north to the plot of land owned by Thomas Palmer, to gawk at his elegant log cabin and swim in the park's fountains and ponds designed by famed landscape architect Frederick Law Olmsted. During race season, the small, fourteen-room resort hotel would fill to capacity as jockeys, owners, and spectators flocked to the Highland Park Racetrack to watch buggy racing in the Michigan sun. The quiet, rural farming town on a ridge had no idea of what lay just fifteen years ahead of it.

When Henry Ford decided his Ford Motor Company and its mechanized tri-umph, the Model T, needed a new facility because they were bursting at the seams of the Ford Piquette Avenue Plant, he purchased 160 acres just north of Manchester Street, between Woodward Avenue and Oakland Street—including land that Cap-tain Stevens had once rented to the Highland Park Resort and racetrack—to build the Highland Park Ford Factory. Hiring the city's most prominent architect, Albert Kahn, he set out to build a factory that would be able to produce cars on a scale the world had never seen. Kahn and his team created a series of large brick and steel buildings over the next ten years. Kahn planned for the expansion of the plant by the connection of additional buildings to meet increased demand in the coming years. His buildings featured large, open spaces that allowed for machines to be arranged to the most efficient configuration. Floor to ceiling windows allowed light to stream in as well as raising the moral of workers often stuck indoors for exhaustingly long hours. When the "Crystal Palace," as the press had dubbed it, was opened in 1910, the world marveled at what had been created. In 1913 the first continuously moving assembly line in the world roared to life in the factory. Miles upon miles of lines, both efficient and devastatingly dangerous to the unwary. Machines capable of pressing out full car panels from single stock sheets of steel. Forge equipment with blistering furnaces. Rivet guns tapping out the factory's pulse. And at its heart, ten thousand workers and a din of mechanical noise so powerful and omnipresent that residents likened it to the coming of a thunder god.

The assembly line's introduction in late winter 1913 achieved a reduction in the assembly time of a Model T from 728 to ninety-three minutes. Nearly eight times quicker to produce and more uniform in production than ever before, the shining black icons of independence rolled off the line. The roaring twenties increased the fever at the plant; in 1920 the plant turned out a car every minute, half of all the automobiles in the world were Model Ts built at Highland Park. Ford stunned the world when he announced a $5 a day wage on January 5, 1914. At the time, workers could count on about $2.25 per day in Detroit. In a single moment Ford became the highest-paying company for manufacturing labor in the world, and also guaranteed every one of its workers could buy a Model T. This was the new Detroit, and in many ways the new America, not yet encumbered by World War II or National Prohibition, and facing unimaginable prosperity. There was Henry Ford, together with the pantheon of early Detroit automotive gods, standing proudly in his kingdom—Highland Park, Detroit.

Ford's political and financial influence is still felt in Highland Park—in fact, it's the only reason Highland Park, like its neighbor to the east, Hamtramck, remained separate from Detroit proper. In 1918, the city was so wealthy due to the taxes paid by not only the factory, but the thousands of wealthy residents who worked for Ford, that they were able to incorporate as a city. Changing from a village to a city was a political move designed to protect the lucrative tax base, as well as to keep Highland Park "desirable" and "clean" from the perceived lower-class city as a whole. The city of Detroit is huge by the standards of most American cities, 142.9 square miles of neighborhoods and enclaves ranging from wealthy to poor, ethnic to regional, old establishment to new boom town. Detroit's ever-expanding boundaries were, undeniably, snapping at the heels of Highland Park and Hamtramck, yet it was their factories—for Hamtramck, Dodge Main, and for Highland Park, the Highland Park Ford Factory—that gave them the might to repeal Detroit's annexation.

During World War II, Highland Park was at the center of the "arsenal of democracy," Roosevelt's plan to arm the Allies in the fight against the Axis powers. At a time when the federal government was, against all odds, trying to out-manufacture the Germans in a come-from-behind victory that was literally do or die, Highland Park was integral. Women wartime workers, like the iconic Rosie the Riveter, flooded into the factories. From 1941 (under Lend-Lease) to 1945, Highland Park and its mixed gender staff built 1,713 Wolverine Tank Destroyers, 1,690 "small hatch" Sherman tanks, trim for nearly 5,000 Jeeps, and 107,803 tents. The tents were in high demand because of the quality to which they were made. The original design was done in the trim shop of Highland Park and their manufacture was not only the cheapest of the war, but also the warmest and most water resistant, earning the women who made them the Army-Navy "E" Award.

In parallel with plant expansion, Highland Park grew, too. In 1910 the village had just over 4,000 residents, but as the Ford Plant expanded throughout the 1910s, the area soon smashed records for population increase when in 1920, 46,500 residents were counted. Louder, larger, and logging more man hours in a day than in the previous century, Highland Park became a mecca for car men and factory workers when Ford was joined in town by the Chrysler Corporation, which was founded in Highland Park in 1925. Chrysler would maintain their world headquarters in the city until 1995. Indeed, when Chrysler left the city under the leadership of Lee Iacocca, 80 percent of the city's remaining tax base left with it.

Today though, an odd architectural relic of Chrysler and Henry Ford's Highland Park often goes unnoticed. Near the old elementary school, concrete tombs sit on each of the street corners. At present they are grated over with heavy metal sheeting that shields the entrance to the underground children's tunnels. Yes, tunnels for children, underground. In the heyday of the city, when taxes were fat and experimentation came in all forms (including urban planning), the city conceived of these subterranean tunnels as a way for school children to cross underneath the street on their way to school, as opposed to battling traffic. After all, Ford's affordable Model T, coupled with high wages, had successfully put an automobile into the hands of nearly every employee. Highland Park boasted one of the highest car ownership rates in the world, and some of the nation's finest schools. So it seemed only natural to play with ways to protect both the human and the hard infrastructures of a city on the rise.

The extent to which Highland Parkers valued innovation and learning was beautifully illustrated when, in 1924, voters approved $500,000 in bonds for a public library. A commission was assembled and sent on a nationwide fact-finding mission to develop a plan for the city's library. Captain Stevens's former home was torn down, and the McGregor Library was built on the land, named to honor the family of Tracy and Katherine (Whitney) McGregor, who years before had converted the home to its orphanage use. When the library was completed in 1926, Highland Park was proud to have nearly three and a half books for every resident, a staggering amount of printed value for any metropolis, let alone an extremely industrialized one. Today the public libraries sit, chained and closed, a tomb for the thousands of books left inside. Current residents flock to a new and novel solution, Little Free Libraries. These tiny birdhouse-style boxes reside all over town. Built by volunteers and erected on private property, they freely exchange books on the honor system. I've cared for one for over a year now on my Highland Park front yard. It supplies nearly seventy-five books a month, most of them children's books.

The city has never been singular in any aspect; it is a study in changes and contrasts. Just as education has gone from some of the best to one of the worst, and books have become a precious commodity given away by private citizens; just as early farmers shared the land, hostilely at times, with Native Americans, and early Christian families shared the village with a racetrack known for its gambling; it's a town of juxtaposition. For all of Ford's rules on the "clean and correct" way to live, there were equally as many proselytizers of the dirty and seedier side of life. Highland Park attracted a range of criminals, from Arthur Lupp, who founded the Black Legion in 1931, ushering in a decade and a half of hate, to a Madam with a heart of gold and business smarts to rival a downtown banker; from a mobster known for running booze, to a man who worked for Henry Ford himself.

Harry Herbert Bennett, the "little man in Henry Ford's basement," was born in Ann Arbor, in 1892. By the age of seventeen, he had joined the United States Navy. A small man at just five foot six inches tall, he was stocky of build. Solid muscle with fire red hair, he was a formidable teenager before the Navy taught him to box. Bennett became a champion lightweight boxer, winning bouts under the name Sailor Reese. He had a reputation for fighting dirty and a reputation for winning. After World War I he met Henry Ford in New York when a newspaper man introduced the red-headed twenty-four-year-old sailor to the automotive icon in a swanky uptown hotel.

Kidnapping extremely rich people and their children was a growing business in America, one that many of Detroit's elite began to fear. Ford was worried about the safety of his son and his grandchildren and had been looking for the right man to protect them. He thought the former sailor was just the man for the job. Bennett was hired at the Highland Park Ford Plant in the art department. Not only did Bennett have no experience in art or design, he had no background in engineering or the automobile business at all. That didn't stop the man from ruthlessly completing Ford's orders. Bennett developed and then led Ford's infamous Service Department. He would break bones, bloody noses, and grease palms in the service of Ford from the basement of the Highland Park Factory. He also had a small shooting range where he and Ford would shoot pistols at pictures of president Franklin Roosevelt. With the full authority of a private police force, Harry Bennett ruled Highland Park, much to the chagrin of fine and honest Ford men like Edsel Ford and Charlie Sorenson, who fought tirelessly to support Roosevelt's Lend-Lease Program and the arsenal of democracy. But, that in and of itself is representative of Highland Park. Whenever it seems a great villain arises, a worthy and equal hero steps into the breach.

But what's a villain without a few henchmen? For Harry Bennett, Highland Park provided an excellent option. Although Highland Park is often lumped in with Detroit in tales of automotive glory or cultural distinction, criminals were keenly aware of its solidarity. For gangsters, bootleggers, and car thieves, Highland Park allowed for the all-important jurisdictional change that felicitated a touch more mischief. During the height of Prohibition, when Detroit imported 75 percent of all the illegal booze coming into America, Highland Park played a central role. Anthony D'Anna, of the famous Sugar House Gang, took up residence in a large Tudor home on a fashionable street, and so effectively evaded the law that he lived to the insanely old mobster age of eighty-four, dying of natural causes. He was known as the "Beer Baron of Detroit" during Prohibition, but later formed lucrative and shady contracts with Harry Bennett, earning himself the moniker Tony "The Car" D'Anna. The deal was simple enough, albeit terrifyingly brutal. In exchange for killing a man, D'Anna would be given a haul-away contract from the Ford Motor Company. This contract allowed him the exclusive right to move cars between the Highland Park factory and the newly operational River Rouge factory. Although records are hard to find, it's nearly certain less than twelve cars were ever moved by D'Anna's E&L Auto Transport, even though the Ford Company paid for thousands. D'Anna's men were present, however, at nearly every union busting, price fixing, and fist fight that Bennett ever instigated.

Sadly, even uglier evils have reared their heads in Highland Park's past as well. The Black Legion was a (not so) secret vigilante group who worked with and at the behest of the Ku Klux Klan. The Klan had already been prominent in Detroit for nearly a decade. The Legion, however, was a smaller, more brutal organization that hated nearly everyone, including immigrants, Catholics, Jews, blacks, labor organizers, and anyone who they felt posed a threat to their perceived idyllic life of yesteryear. To the great shame of the city, several public officials, including the chief of police, a mayor, and a city councilman, along with business owners and respected community members, joined up. Murder, kidnappings, and a reign of terror are the legacy of the group, and cut a deep scar through the city's proud history. Eventually, Lupp and forty-seven men were indicted following the murder of Charles Poole in May 1936; Lupp and ten others were convicted. Shockingly, the investigation brought about as a result of the Poole murder found that the Legion had been involved in numerous other murders or conspiracies to murder during the previous three years. Thirty-seven additional men were convicted and jailed for their involvement, effectively ending the fifteen year reign of the Legion.

This duality of spirit isn't just between right and wrong, but also sometimes between wrong and wrong in Highland Park's history. Although firmly on the wrong side of the law, another resident was bending, breaking, and altogether flagrantly destroying the rules, yet her good heart and shrewd business sense have earned her an enduring respect and bourgeois reputation for those in the know around Detroit. Bringing her name up in some long-established bars will result in men of a certain age cracking knowing smiles, and every now and then a story worthy of a screenplay. For a woman with a forty-year tenure as a resolute criminal, she spent a relatively short time in Highland Park. But boy, did she make the best of them.

Helen McGowan, more famously Helen "Rocking Chair" McGowan, was "The Motor City Madam"; the brilliant businesswoman, author, kindly-souled, dirty-mouthed madam of Detroit's finest brothels, from the mid-1930s to 1965. Later she penned a tell-all book, one of the first of its kind, *Motor City Madam* (since reprinted as *Big City Madam*), that outed many a Detroit mover and shaker, and forever cemented her into Detroit lore.

That she moved to Highland Park, in the middle of World War II when the Ford factory was producing M4A3 Sherman tanks as fast as it could and the population had swelled to accommodate workers, was not a mistake. She was known to move regularly, boasting, "I lived in over 300 houses during my forty years in Detroit. When John Law came knocking, I was damn sure no one was home to answer." An older Detroit gentleman described Helen's scheme to me as "the worst kept secret in Detroit." "When you saw her name in the paper you knew she'd gone and moved shop, and you knew there was only one thing she was selling." Helen, under her original birth name Mae Absliter, her married name Mae Jullian, and under her more infamous moniker, greeted clients, avoided the cops, and learned the secrets of the city. Perhaps because of her notoriety, or perhaps because World War II was raging and the police just had better things to do, she was able to stay in the Highland Park, nearly double the next longest stay she ever had, and way longer than her seven-week average.

The Motor City Madame's journey to Highland Park is a tale within itself. After a heartbreakingly sad and bizarre early life that lead her from the sharecropping fields of Missouri where she was born, into Al Capone's Cotton Club in Chicago, Mae made her way to Detroit via train, bus, and hitchhiking. Arriving to a rewrite on the classic model of prostitution, in which the whore made less money than the pimp, and dirty cops and racket boys sold them to willing customers, and promised brutal retribution for noncompliance. After a fateful meeting with a student desperate for cash to finish his studies, Mae—now rechristened Helen to camouflage her Chicago past—hatched a plan to fund his education in return for half of his income post-graduation. The plan came to fruition and by 1933, Helen "Rocking Chair" McGowan was chain smoking Pall Mall cigarettes, rocking slowly in her chair, and observantly vetting each man in and out of her very own brothel. She adored her girls and fiercely protected them; paying for doctors, manicurists, and hairstylists to come to the houses, she cared for their needs while protecting her stock. She claimed to never pay off cops because they'd arrest her anyhow and slap on an extortion charge to boot, yet plenty of sweat-soaked rolls of bills slipped from her mighty bosom into the hands of officers, just not in the way you'd think. Helen was famous for her relationships with lawmen; she even dedicated her book to them in 1964. Arrested enough times to know every officer in Detroit, Highland Park, and Hamtramck, she was famous for buying all of their fundraising field day tickets and then giving them away to local kids. She revolutionized the treatment and care of her girls, and such a reputation attracted the finest women in the United States and Canada to her service. Girls from the South would come via train on tickets charged to her account in order to be interviewed; local beauty queens down on their luck, drug addicts who had known no other way of life, and even one socialite who needed some marital revenge, found their way to Helen. Helen's tenure in Highland Park ended under a veil of mystery, moves, and possibly an arrest, but by 1944 she had to return to her girls and the next house. A woman who broke so many laws in Detroit that new ones were written specifically to fill loopholes she'd found. Kind and generous, gutsy and no nonsense. A naked, foul-mouthed Robin Hood for the ages, and a proud Highland Parker. In 1957 she wrote a letter to a friend: "I've known good areas and bad areas.

Good people and bad people. H. P. (Highland Park) has the best of both."

Juxtaposed against all of the good and all of the bad of Highland Park's history, the city has come upon hard times in the last fifty years. Ford Motor Company moved to Dearborn and began to end production at its Highland Park plant in the late 1950s. The city suffered the loss of skilled and unskilled trade jobs in parallel with Detroit and Hamtramck. Massive declines in population and tax base were accompanied by an increase in street crime. Suburban flight from the city accelerated after the 1967 Detroit riots. Ford's last operation at the factory was the production of tractors. That ended in 1973, and a year later, the entire property was sold to a private developer for general industrial use. Chrysler, the last major private sector employer in the city, moved its corporate headquarters from Highland Park to Auburn Hills in the 1990s. They paid the city $44 million in corporate compensation and unfilled municipal contracts. As the final 6,000 or so Chrysler employees left for good, the restaurants, bars, and shops that had supported their lunch hours and after-work activities suffered.

Today, Highland Park is often mistaken for a neighborhood, like the Cass Corridor or Grandmont Rosedale. The conventional wisdom of "people outside of Detroit are scared of Detroit; people inside of Detroit are scared of Highland Park" has become the blustering, unofficial city slogan. Today some of the factory's "crystal palace" buildings have found new life as discount clothing stores, or been torn down to make way for grocery stores and fast food chains, although recent buying interest has been considerably more varied, from an artist in residency group to a German nightclub. Yet Highland Park is here, and has as much love, interest, whimsy, and possibly more history than perhaps any part of the Motor City.

Just a block past the old Ford Factory on Victor Street, down the road from the now defunct Acme Photographic, which all but invented automotive photography in the 1920s, you'll find two culinary gems. Stop in to Red Hots Coney Island, an institution since 1921. Originally owned by the Nickolson family, Greeks who immigrated to Detroit and opened the dinner to cater to the overflowing workers of the plant when a Model T rolled off the line every minute. Men like Edsel Ford, Charles Sorenson, and the despicable Harry Bennett were common sights in the neighborhood. The diner became famous for its homemade chili sauce, affordable breakfasts, and friendly, fast service. Its popularity increased so much that by the mid-twenties a system was developed where shift change at the plant meant lines of brown paper bags with two coney dogs in each covered the counter. Hungry lineworkers would walk in, grab a bag (or three), and drop their money in a small box on the honor system. By the 1940s a cousin of the original owners had taken over and managed to secure a lucrative, if not humongous, new contract—Red Hots was employed to feed the prisoners at the nearby Highland Park Police Station on a daily basis. Coney dogs and egg sandwiches were delivered to cells and guards alike over the next decades as Ford men, Highland Parkers, and municipal workers lined up for the iconic food.

In the 1960s the establishment changed hands when Gene and Norris bought it and ran it with the help of their young son Richard. The recipes have stayed the same, and new menu items—along with beer—have been added. Today you can still find the family smiling at their diner; Richard is grown up, and his wife Carol works at Red Hots with him. Half cooking and serving, half following a routine they've perfected over nearly fifty years. They'll fix you a fantastic breakfast, share the street gossip, laugh about the Lions, celebrate the Tigers, and welcome you. Order the Detroit classic, a coney dog with chopped white onions and yellow mustard, topped with their original recipe chili. The breakfasts are great—flat top griddle American classics served with grits or homefries, and blazing hot, for less than five bucks. The place still fills up with locals: cops, firemen, and laborers. If you're lucky, you'll catch Rich and Carol's daughter Christina waitressing, and she'll make you a Vernor's Float with a splash of maraschino cherry juice that'll knock your socks off.

Next door to Red Hots is Victor's Bakery. It's an old school Polish establishment that's run by a band of women as fiercely culinarily traditional as they are ethnically diverse. African American, Polish, Ukrainian, and just plain Highland Park proud, the bakers open shop at seven in the morning after three previous hours of labor. A slice of their sweet potato cake will set you back a mere buck and a quarter, but the towering and moist coffee cake will linger in your mind until you find your way back. Patrons carry white paper boxes out by the stack, and the birthday cake business has changed little over the last seventy-five years, although the character requests have shifted from Superman to the Incredible Hulk and onward, in accordance with the newest movie or latest trend. Day-old cookies can be had by the dozen for pocket change, and although the hours are until 5:00 p.m., it's worth calling ahead, as they often sell out and close up shop early on busy days.

On Woodward you'll find Nandi's Knowledge Café, a sandwich shop, coffee bar, and bookshop, among other things. They trade in African American books, ranging from religious to historical, single-print staple-bound, from local authors to classics like Dr. King's speeches. The Knowledge Café is also home to serious chess games, Islamic prayer meetings, and anything else Nidia feels needs a home. Some days that means wandering into her tin-roofed shop to a pelting of questions about racial issues, gentrification, or public education. Sometimes it means accidentally interrupting a drum circle class or poetry reading. In a fashion harkening back to the old school business antics of small town Detroit, next door her stepdaughter operates a vintage shop that caters to women looking for that perfect fifty-year-old hat or vintage bag. In a city with less than 65 percent commercial occupancy, any building block occupied by two locally owned shops and a cellular store feels hopeful.

Amongst the century club businesses of Highland Park, the Becharas Brothers Coffee Company sits proudly at the head of the table (or at least stands tall serving the coffee). Opened in 1914 by two European brothers, the coffee roasters have supplied most of the coffee you've been drinking around Detroit without you ever knowing it, due to their ubiquitous commercial contracts. For half a century, the Becharas supplied the coffee to the Elias Brothers' Big Boy restaurants, multiple car dealerships, independent diners like Red Hots Coney Island, and the mass orders of the United States military. The family still owns the company, and today it's overseen by the grandchildren. Widely considered one of the finest large-scale coffee roasters in the nation, they've recently begun selling their signature blends directly to the public via their website. Whether you view a hundred-year-old coffee roaster's entrance into e-commerce with delight or dismay, it's a sign of new life in the city.

As Highland Park and the people who proudly proclaim it home move into the future, I'm proud to be one of them, although in many ways I'm far more interested in its past. I smile when my truck scares up the local pheasants, or news of beavers returning to local streams and park ponds fill the local diners' evening conversation. As a native Detroiter, I'm far more familiar with the west side Warrendale neighborhood where my family has lived for almost 100 years. I had grown accustomed to the University District where I attended college and the west side comforts of family and familiar haunts. But in 2015, after an exhaustive hunt for the perfect building to house my dream project, I landed in an area of town I had never considered. I came to Highland Park for a home that so cleanly wraps up the history of Detroit through decades of owners that the conceit of its cliché is staggering. Completed in 1916 by an executive at the Ford Highland Park Plant, the home resides on a wide, pedestrian-friendly street, of the sort any family of the early 1900s would envy. It sits kitty-corner to the home built by Tony "The Car" DeAnna, who ran booze for the Sugar House and Purple Gangs during Prohibition, and who later had lucrative deals with Harry Bennett's Ford goons to beat in a few heads in the anti-union fights of the 1930s and 1940s. It transferred ownership a few more times and had a front row seat to still more history, owing to the area's involvement with the KKK's Black Legion in the 1930s and the block's involvement with the Black Panthers in the 1960s. Neighbors proudly tell the story of the yellow house at the end of the block that once hosted Dr. Martin Luther King Jr. for dinner after being secured by Walter Reuther for his Detroit stay, although I've never been able to substantiate the claim, and have to admit it's most likely the sort of oral history run amuck that historians both love and despise.

But now it's transforming again; like the century-old coffee roaster who now sells online, this hundred-year-old gem is finding a new life as the headquarters of Detroit History Tours and the Detroit History Club. As it undergoes the transformation into a home that will welcome members for monthly dinners and historical lectures, it teaches me daily that Highland Park is here, storied and rich in history. It's a city within a city; a place where good, hard-working folks can find a hot breakfast, a bookstore debate, a friendly slice of sweet potato cake, or a fascinating bit of history—if they just know where to look, along the short span of stoplights on Woodward Avenue.

# Long Live the City of Trees

*Marsha Music*

## PROLOGUE

*I* wrote this homage to my hometown for our Facebook group of Black, tail-end baby-boomer Highland Parkers—and our White schoolmates. Whites who had left the city as children with their parents' "flight," and now, more than forty years later, had begun to find us and gravitate to the group. We reminisced about our growing up in the verdant, prosperous city that we remembered, and I began to capture my thoughts about the city that I love.

§

I call myself a "primordial Detroiter" and a "Detroitist"—but actually I was born in Detroit and, after about age three, raised in Highland Park. I grew up on California Street, on the corner of John R, in a stucco, Mission-style behemoth—all oak beams and leaded glass on a beautiful block of giant Arts & Crafts homes.

Woodward Avenue was the center of my universe, and John R my most beloved thoroughfare.

Highland Park, not quite three square miles, is one of the two cities (Hamtramck is the other) that actually lie within the physical boundaries of Detroit—a "city within a city." One of the premier municipalities of the mid-twentieth century, Highland Park was subsequently regarded by some as the epicenter of the Detroit area's economic decline. But I recall the days when Highland Park was officially spoken of as an affluent "suburb" of Detroit, with the elevated societal position that the term implied.

I love Highland Park.

## THE CITY OF TREES

There have been many conversations among present and former Highland Park-ers expressing the contradiction between our great memories of growing up in the city and the reality of the crime, poverty, decay, and craziness that afflicted much of our town in the decades since. Entire blocks of solid homes have reverted back to nature, and Hamilton Avenue, a six-lane street built wide from the old days of workday traffic, is today mostly bedraggled and barren. Yet several blocks of the city's legendary housing stock remain intact and stately, the historic bungalows exemplars of architectural Americana. Some of us are deeply ambivalent about H. P., and for good reason.

We grew up in what was one of the most prosperous and successful mid-century cities in the United States. We are products of the best that could be granted to us in our lifetime. Because of the automotive industry and many of our parents' rela-tionship to it, tiny Highland Park was a microcosm of mid-century Americana, and among the first cities to reflect the proletarian affluence born of the auto industry that later came to be called the modern middle-class.

We are the repositories of the best that public education of the last century could yield; we are the last Detroit-area generation that enjoyed a relative affluence at the peak of industrial society; we are the realized dreams of the people who came before us who had nothing but prayer and work ethic to bequeath to their seed.

We have always felt "different" than those born and raised in the city that sur-rounded us, and some of us are the most literate, articulate, political, entrepreneurial, musical people born of working-class life in the North. We who grew up there during certain years are also people who experienced, for a brief period, real integration.

We grew up in a lush green city; rain could barely reach the sidewalks beneath the canopy of Dutch Elms arching over the streets of our hometown. Although there were many plain frame houses in the city, Highland Park houses, on many of the streets, were magnificent, especially on the "state" streets—Connecticut, California, Rhode Island, Massachusetts, Colorado—where I grew up, along with McLean and Farrand Park; and on the streets that formed an enclave of arts and crafts bungalows in the city's North End; Puritan, Eason, and Moss.

There is no small irony in the fact that some of these homes that our parents pur-chased, through much labor and sacrifice, rivaled the plantation homes of the South, in the shadows of which some of them once worked and lived.

Oak walls, room-sized mantles over fireplaces, stained glass, French doors, lead-ed glass, carved bannisters, beamed ceilings—some, if not all of these architectural elements were present in even some of the most modest Highland Park homes. We were often surprised when others referred to our houses as "historic," for growing up in Mission-style elegance and Arts and Crafts beauty was simply the norm—in fact, most of us didn't even know these names for the aesthetic conditions in which we lived.

Our parents, many from the segregated South, were the visionaries who foresaw the benefits of having their children grow up in a city that at the time had one of the best school systems in the country, and surely the best in the state. Many adults in our midst were professionals, artists, and creative people, including educated Black folks who had seen many limitations to success in their pre-Highland Park lives.

In the 1950s and '60s, many whites chose to leave upon our arrival or, rather, were driven out by a fear of blacks drummed into their households—especially by real estate and development interests that stood to gain by the rapid turnover of houses at the time. Some stayed for a time, and, in fact, there were some Whites and other nationalities that came to live in Highland Park during those years because it was integrated. As adults, many of the city's children are been uniquely situated in the world, with more inclusive and expansive attitudes and experiences than others, because of growing up in Highland Park.

There are generations of Highland Parkers—whites who grew up in the forties and fifties, for whom "our" coming was the signal for their family's exodus. There are those who came after—post-seventies Blacks who did not have the benefit of the standard of living that we enjoyed, who came to H. P. after the collapse and/or flight of the industries and paychecks that supported the city. Both of these groups have different experiences in H. P. than did we.

Highland Park was ground zero for the collapse of the auto industry and the changes in industrial America. The fall of its tax base, the Vietnam-era penetration of heroin into the community, and a generation later, crack cocaine—and the social mayhem that resulted from both—was a horrific layer of social misery that spelled the end of a way of life.

Many of us have suffered, having grown up in middle-class stability, yet seeing the next generations struggle in the economics of decline. But as Highland Park has gone, so goeth others;  new cities and suburban communities—Black and White— are now experiencing the economic and social challenges for which our city was first in line.


## THE "OVERNIGHT" CHANGE

Contrary to popular narrative, the movement of Whites out of Highland Park and Detroit did not begin with the '67 riots—a.k.a. rebellion—that ignited in Detroit, but was a process that had begun in the postwar 1940s—long before Blacks became a majority. But due to the amazing housing stock of Highland Park and its vastly superior school system, I believe that many whites held on in that city longer than those in Detroit, giving Highland Park an experience of integration, in certain neighborhoods, for longer than in its surrounding city.

The Highland Park in which I grew up was a United Nations of children, with parents from many lands. Many of our black parents were pleased that they had acquired for their children, through untold challenges, the living embodiment of the

American Dream. My first experience in welcoming a new neighbor came before first grade, when I walked four doors down and met tiny Mrs. Yushiko Hoagland from Japan, who introduced me to her two biracial children, Cecily and Kim—and we are friends to this day.

The kids in my old Barber Middle School were from families from Lebanon, China, Armenia, Iraq, and numbers of White children whose parents had not yet moved away. We played together, often unaware that the racial maelstrom in the South—that swirled around our young minds, emanating from the TV news—was real, though less visible, in Highland Park, too.

For sure, the parents of my young White friends had many reasons for moving other than race. Many of the new suburbs outside of the Eight Mile Road boundary of Detroit (two miles from Highland Park) transformed from virtual farmland in some cities to bright new communities seemingly overnight, as factories moved and civic promoters and developers promoted the joys of suburbia.

The powerful lure of new, modern homes with modern amenities was an attractive incentive for families facing the prospect of long years ahead in the big old homes of Highland Park, most of which had been built from 1900 to the 1920s—and, by the fifties and sixties, needed costly repairs.

But, undoubtedly, race also played a great and obvious role, exacerbating all the other elements of what came to be known as white flight. Despite statements as to why the city changed "overnight" without open racial conflict, well, there was racial tension in Highland Park. But we were children, and mostly children get along—the adults are the problems.

I recall that in the early sixties, when Highland Park was still majority White, there was a bunch of mean, older White guys who made it clear that my little brown friends and I were not welcome, especially at the ice skating rink near the old Henry Ford Plant (which housed the first auto assembly line in the country). The great pop song by Lou Christie, "Lightnin' Strikes," will forever be linked with my memories of circling the ice, trying to avoid the snarling bullies spitting the N-word who loomed like monsters over us.

I remember my brother and I being called that word by White neighbor children on California Street during a routine kids' squabble over our backyard fences. We were stunned; we had been friends all of our young lives—but we had the feeling that it was the adults in their household who were behind the kids' changing attitudes, and for sure, soon they moved to the suburbs.

By the seventies, drugs and crime were paramount in the changing city. I recall Mrs. Naomi Oden, a gentle but fierce Rosa Parks-ian pillar of Cortland Street, before her family moved several blocks north to an Arts & Crafts masterpiece on Puritan. She was a spiritual woman of the Baha'i faith, who was prophetic in her zealous exhortations on the coming of the scourge of drugs.

I had no idea, as a ninth grader in 1968, that her passionate, agonized warnings on her front porch spoke much about what was to come, though later it was clear that she was right. Criminality began to overcome the town that was not prepared to hold its barricades against the new, deadly, drug-fueled forces. "Mama Oden" and her husband, John Oden Sr., both now deceased, were prophetic trailblazers who went on to found the drug treatment center Elmhurst Home (on Linwood, in Detroit), and are memorable for their tireless work against the scourge of drugs that began to permeate Highland Park—and Detroit.

However, the most important element in the change of the racial dynamics of Highland Park was the decline in the economic infrastructure. There was an extraordinary amount of industry and jobs for such a tiny city, including Ford's first assembly plant, Chrysler's world headquarters, and more. In the early days, many of the employees of these companies lived in the city—and in fact, a large segment of the beautiful homes of Highland Park were built for Henry Ford's managerial class.

When the Ford plant no longer operated and, years later, when Chrysler headquarters and other industry subsidiaries (like Excello) closed, their (mostly White) employees who lived in Highland Park also moved. This factor alone was significant in its contribution to so-called White flight, and a catastrophic end to the taxes that these companies had provided to subsidize the "good life" in what had been a lush, prosperous city. Over time, as unemployment and layoffs from the Big Three began to be the rule and not the cyclical exception, the taxes and income that had helped to support the city and maintain the homes and neighborhoods were decimated as well.

## BLACK MAYBERRY

There is a very specific set of memories and experiences of those of us who lived in the City of Trees, and a need for affirmation that we probably didn't even know that we had. We have lived our lives—some in the metropolitan area of Detroit, some on the coasts of this country and cities in between, some in the far reaches of the earth, and some still, in Highland Park—feeling that we are "different."

I described our upbringing to an interviewer once as a sort of Black *Mayberry RFD*, a TV show about a fictional small town. Our identity was clearly separate from Detroit. But it was really much more than that. I cannot emphasize enough the unique and powerful economic and social convergence that was Highland Park. Our community defined the middle class. But because Highland Park became majority Black, this reality became obscured and/or denied. The tainted view of the city that paints its past with the brush of its current condition robs both the Black and White former residents of the city of an accurate view of the former grandeur of the town that we all remember—and its role in history.

Today, our old neighborhoods hold on in a facsimile of their former grandeur, the efforts of generations to hold on clearly in evidence. During my growing up, the neighborhood was abuzz with lawnmowers and hedge-cutters; homes were in a constant cycle of sprucing up and repair. Kids tried unsuccessfully to escape their parent's perpetual lists of chores and cleanup demands and only my siblings' duty at our father's record shop kept our lists of tasks at bay.

Our across-the-street-neighbors, the Davises, were relentless in keeping up their home, their weekends spent planting, weeding, and painting trim—and fifty years later, a look at their still lovely home and landscape shows their toil was not in vain. We'd see Mr. Claude Harvard, a tall, brown man who ceaselessly cut his grass on the corner of Connecticut and John R, and marveled at his surgical precision with a mower and lawn tools (few of us knew that he was a mathematics genius and a skilled inventor who received recognition for his work with Henry Ford, a rare acknowledgment for a Black man in those times). Such pride in home ownership was common, though there are those who wrongfully believe that we Blacks lived in a state of disarray and disrepair.

With the rise of the prosperity of the middle class (industrial, service, and municipal workers; educators and other professionals), so rose the lives of those of us who lived among the green lawns and oaken homes of Highland Park. Since the roots of the American industrial economy were nurtured on our verdant soil, Highland Park was, in a de facto sense, a beacon of "the good life" to many other municipalities.

Ironically, the concentration of capital was so pronounced that a radical labor organization, the nemesis of segregated practices in the auto industry and in the UAW—the League of Revolutionary Black Workers—was headquartered in Highland Park on Cortland Street and Third, a place for much post-sixties activism and a center for radical intellectuals like auto worker General Baker, who remained a Highland Park resident until his death in 2014. His widow, Marian Kramer, is an activist for the poor and unemployed, and has turned her focus to the struggles over water rights, which are an acute issue in Highland Park and Detroit, due to the municipal crisis in the city.

Though much of Highland Park living can be described as idyllic, the pangs of racial prejudice and inequities were real, and sixties protests became as much a part of the fabric of the city as in Detroit during those times. The Wheelers, Earl and Naomi, were den parents to our youthful protests against less than equal treatment in the schools, and they remained active elders in the community.

As the underpinnings of the city's economic foundation began to collapse, so did life as we knew it. As Highland Park faltered, so did other cities' downward municipal spirals. I recall how Highland Park was reviled by pundits in the first years of its economic reversals; yet today, reduced and shared police and firefighters, shrinking school districts, and lack of services have become a reality in many cities.

Many Highland Parkers grew up with unusually large, beautiful homes on lush, green streets, and even those who did not were beneficiaries of an exemplary primary and secondary public education. We had quintessential American childhoods, racially integrated for a time (I was one of a less than a handful of black children in Mrs. Dorothy Ashford's first grade). We had full-size swimming pools in middle school, a YMCA and YWCA, an unmatched musical education that nurtured innumerable talented musicians and a national-award-winning marching band; intramural sports, ice skating, clubs, scouts, and a plethora of cultural and athletic activities that would rival any private school system—then or today.

For sure, though, although some White teachers were delighted to have classrooms with a rainbow of children, others treated us—and our parents—with ill-disguised prejudice and disdain; but we were able to learn around them, anyway. There were Black teachers, some of whom had come from the segregated systems of the South and were especially dedicated to excellence in education and deportment, as well—I note Mrs. Elizabeth Banton, teacher of Latin and the Classics, a paragon of scholarship.

Additionally, there was a memorable shopping district on Woodward Avenue, anchored by Kresge's and Sears, that made it unnecessary to shop anywhere else and relegated downtown Detroit's merchants' row to an optional retail experience. We had the magnificent, golden-doored McGregor Library on Woodward (with a giant globe and dollhouse within, and amazing "stereoscopic" hand-held viewers) that nurtured the minds of countless residents—and, during difficult times in my young life—was my home away from home.

Our Highland Park community of color has rarely been heralded or discussed in terms other than negative, as if only Whites had solid, productive, middle-class lives—but for sure, we did. It is likewise as if White people were incapable of having growing-up experiences with Blacks that produced memorable, happy childhoods—but for sure, they did. Despite the later collapse of the city as we knew it, history and memories affirm the realities of our upbringing that have rarely been acknowledged.

During my teen years, Highland Park's mayor was Robert "Bob" Blackwell, as light-skinned and straight-haired as a White man—and a Republican; the first Black mayor in the U.S. and the only Black Republican mayor. This was noteworthy in the days of the Kennedy dynasty, but I note that many Black elders of the time still held allegiance with the party of Lincoln during a time when segregation in the South was championed by Southern Democrats who came to be called "Dixiecrats" (and millions of federal funds funneled into the city via the mayor's amiable connections with President Nixon contributed to the comfort of the city as well).

Election Day in Highland Park was a Rockwellian affirmation of enfranchisement, in marked contrast to the televised mayhem of attacks on Blacks trying to vote in the South. I remember proudly walking to the polls at McGregor Library on Election Days with my pretty Mama and being greeted by the colored ladies who, on these special days, were the all-important poll workers—some of whom doubtless had relatives in the South in harm's way for even thinking hard about voting. For the adults in our lives in Highland Park, Election Day was serious, indeed.

Our neighbor, Mrs. Jean Green, the first Black city clerk of Highland Park, was a smart, no-nonsense, beauty-shop owner and businesswoman from Highland Park's "North-End," a poorer section of the city that had been majority Black long before the rest of the city. She was an exemplar of electoral prowess and a mentor of countless students and professionals, who excelled nationwide. The old Caucus Club was an electoral power center, the African American version of the old-time Rotary Clubs.

Despite political upheavals, rivalries, chicanery, and outright corruption in the small-town politics of Highland Park, empowerment was a reality in that town long before that word became popular.

## A HIGHLAND PARK RESURRECTION

The old days of Highland Park, with a standard of living based on the wages of industrial workers, is over. That way of life was the result of economic forces that no longer exist in the city, and from a culture that emerged from our parents' upbringings—mostly in the South and varied countries of origin.

But I believe because of the unique attributes of the city—its location near a hub of freeways and near the core of Detroit, its remaining housing stock still intact and much of it substantial, its commercial areas—this is not a city that will just "ride off into the sunset" and into nonexistence.

We Highland Parkers of a certain age are the first generation to experience the full realization of the American Dream that began with our parents in the South, in Black Bottom, in the Old Country. But by the same token, since the economic tsunami subsequently began in Highland Park, we are also the last generation to experience the type of urban middle-class life that we had amongst some of the highest-paid working people in history in one small concentrated town. If we are both the first and last, we are therefore, the only ones to have experienced life in quite the special way that we did in Highland Park—and that's why we feel so "different."

A new Highland Park could develop in a few short years, and soon—depending of the needs of developers, mass transit, and so on. We may not see it in our lifetimes. But it will happen. In a Highland Park of the future, those who held on and stayed —despite all—may be the only Blacks who will be able to afford to live there—and, with water bill problems, foreclosures, and high restoration costs, even they are increasingly challenged to hold on. For in most "reborn" communities, housing prices become a premium and moneyed folks become the only ones able to afford gentrified homes and land.

There are still beautiful houses and dedicated homeowners and residents who await the day that the city's decline will plateau, and its stable blocks will be returned to their former grandeur. The school system has, shockingly, been effectively dismantled. But I believe the day of the phoenix is coming—at least for the sections of the city that are still intact. It is the cyclical nature of things, and the underlying needs of investors in land capital.

Yes, Woodward Avenue, or even devastated Hamilton, may yet be a place of new shops and galleries. Yes, our Arts & Crafts bungalows, Mission-style and stone houses may yet be coveted and rise in price to their real value. Yes, there may be redeveloped commercial areas.

Our descendants will not, in the main, be the inheritors of the lives that we had there; others, most of whom know little about how we lived in Highland Park, will reap the benefits of generations of care. The proletarian affluence of working-class Black people and the way we lived back in the day may become only a memory in Highland Park, a time and place that existed for a historical moment and, like a vapor, will disappear into the ether. This makes the recounting of our history in Highland Park tantamount—so that it will never be said that we did not exist, that our way of life was but a dream.

Highland Park—at least the sections of it that remain intact and retain their architectural loveliness—will carry on. For there are those who have held on despite all; new investors will surely alight upon the City of Trees, and, most importantly, the fervent prayers of the righteous who once dwelled there, and those who still do —availeth much.

I love Highland Park.


## EPILOGUE

The stucco Mission-style home in which I grew up burned in an electrical fire in 2007 and I left Highland Park.

Activists are building enclaves of creativity on Avalon Street, and substantial urban farms are ensconced on land where I once visited friends in their homes. In 2015, Galapagos Art Center in Brooklyn announced plans to relocate to the old, vacant, Highland Park High School/Community College campus—where I used to attend (and skip) school back in the day.

On Midland, west of Hamilton, the obscure street of old light industrial buildings makes a curve, revealing a massive factory turned art gallery—host to new "Big Art Shows," drawing hundreds of artists and enthusiasts to a decimated area of Highland Park.

In a city where most of the light poles were literally repossessed for lack of municipal payment, young thinkers and doers are developing solar lighting. The amazing Arts & Crafts homes of Highland Park are gaining renewed appreciation through historic architectural websites and online groups, and people—including creatives —are moving into them. The phoenix is rising.

My husband and I recently purchased a house in the North End of Detroit, near my beloved John R, and blocks away from the home I grew up in, in Highland Park.

# Six Mile, Dexter, Plymouth, Gratiot, and Grand River

*Lhea J. Love*

I always loved
the way bus drivers
tip their heads as if hats
every time another driver
passes by.

It is as if they are part of
a secret fraternal order
of beautiful Black men:

a secret society
of men dealing with
underpaid workers, unwed mothers
struggling to fold, struggling to force
baby carriages beneath seats
and out of aisle ways;
dealing with unruly teenagers
miseducated and misinformed
by a failing school system
that never expected anything
of them anyhow;
dealing with homeless men
and homeless women
using green bus tickets with a transfer
to get them to the nearest shelter
warming center or soup kitchen
where they won't be alone;
dealing with the rightfully
angry, the permanently intoxicated,
the long-term drug-addicted soul
who needs something
other than themselves
to evade the harshness
of their reality.

I always loved
the way bus drivers
greeted each other
in any moment
on any street
at any turn

acknowledging that Black love
is Black wealth, Black people
are Black power and Black
community is the only family
we'll ever know.

And I thank God
for every bow and every wave,
every smile and every hello

that gets me from where I am in my hood
to where, in my future, I need to go.

—*previously published by* Third Wednesday, *a literary journal in Ann Arbor, Michigan*

# A Home in Russell Woods

*Jill Day*

*W*hen the time came to respond to the longing to put down roots, to leave apartment living and create a space and place for my family, I really had more of a feeling of what I sought rather than a checklist. Okay, yeah, I had certain expectations as far as the number of bedrooms, bathrooms, and other amenities, but I also sought what would feel like home as well. This was going to be the place that would be my retreat, a place of refuge and restoration for my sons and me. The task was to find not just a house, but a neighborhood that would feel like home.

My introduction to Russell Woods was like meeting someone with whom there's an immediate connection. If Russell Woods had been an actual person, he would have been that guy who's popular without effort, that combination of cool, old-school assuredness with just the right amount of new-school swagger. It had a little something for everyone—elders with whom my mom could reminisce, classmates who had grown up with my sons, and a mix of young adults who moved through the same professional and social circles as mine. The house itself embodied all of the cherished memories of home during my upbringing with the adult accoutrements I needed to embrace the life I had created.

It had been an arduous search to not only find the right house, but to find the right neighborhood. While I was familiar with the neighborhoods of my youth, both in the city and the suburbs, I was determined to make my home in the city of my birth. I love Detroit. I mean, I love Detroit! Don't get me wrong because, with few exceptions, every place I've lived holds a special place in my heart. But nowhere can ever replace or take the place of the Motor City. There was an inexplicable hold the city had over me, I had to live here. It was as if my life depended on it. The challenge was to find somewhere that would nurture my growing family and provide the environment that would equip my sons to face the world.

The neighborhoods of my youth had changed drastically or had been completely eradicated by the ravages of time and circumstance. The riots of '67, white flight to the suburbs and flight of young professionals from the Rust Belt, lows of the auto industry, escalating crime rates that resulted in the seemingly unshakeable "Murder Capital" title (which was and is so much more applicable to many other cities like Washington, D.C., Philadelphia, Los Angeles, New York, New Orleans, and Chicago), the drug epidemic, the economy, and shrinking workplace made house hunting exhausting. I learned all too well the realtor mantra of "Location, location, location!" and its impact on my quest. Although the locales I once knew so well were no longer viable options, I still sought the emotional connection they evoked. I couldn't put my finger on it and was at a loss as to how to explain it, but I'd know it when I found it.

Since their arrival in Detroit from Alabama and South Carolina, my parents' families took up residence on the east side, with my maternal side in Grixdale Park/ Conant Gardens and my paternal side in the North End. Although I loved the location and the Chrysler Elementary School for my elder son that drove my selecting my apartment in Lafayette Park, I wanted more space, a yard, and just having something of my own that wasn't available on my budget in my then locale.

One of my friends ended up being my neighborhood matchmaker, so to speak as she was starting her own house-hunting journey. After striking out with a few west side candidates as well as some east side contenders, she mentioned that another friend of hers had just moved within her neighborhood. The community was stable and homes virtually never hit the market as they were usually passed down or sold via word of mouth. The owner, a widower, had died and none of his children wanted the home. Word was that maybe one of the nieces, nephews, or cousins might want it, or the possibility of renting it was also being considered. His sister lived at the end of the next block and she happened to be one of my sorority sisters.

As I drove up and down the blocks of Russell Woods, my excitement mounted. I was more and more impressed with what I saw and how it made me feel. I didn't want to wait until I got home to call my friend to find out if the family was willing to sell it. I did something I saw in the movie, *The War of the Roses*, and quickly wrote two notes. I asked that if the family ever wanted to sell the house, to please contact me to give me the first opportunity to place a bid. I placed one in the home's mailbox and the other in the sister's. Within the week I was contacted by the executor of the owner's estate and a few months later I was a homeowner.

The best thing about Russell Woods was and is its fostering of community. Maybe because it tends to focus on families, whether it's keeping homes within them, or how welcoming others on the block were, or simply how the neighbors looked out for each other. A strong block club, free jazz concerts in the neighborhood park, and the foundation of the relationships make Russell Woods both one of Detroit's best kept secrets and my favorite home because it allows my sons to have the same love of community that I cherished from my upbringing.

# Minock Park

## *Erin Marquis*

*T*he first month I lived in Minock Park, my new neighbors would stop while I tackled the endless yard work to introduce themselves and always had the same reaction. I'd watch as a look of surprise and maybe mild amusement would cross their faces. They would then shrug and smile and give a warm introduction. The interaction would always end the same way—with phone numbers exchanged and a serious, heartfelt promise: "We look out for each other here."

I lost count of how many times I heard that phrase in my first few months of owning a home in Minock Park. As for the shocked faces, I understood their initial disbelief. Minock Park is the smallest neighborhood in Grandmont-Rosedale, a collection of five neighborhoods on the northwest side of the city. It's not hip. Here, homes range from stately, five-bedroom brick beauties to crumbling cinder-block shacks with sagging, corrugated tin roofs. There aren't any bars, or farm-to-table restaurants. There are about 1,200 people in tiny Minock Park, the vast majority of whom are black.

Now I've lived here less than a year. I'm no expert on the flavor of all five neighborhoods. But from what I've observed, it was my age that surprised my neighbors more than the color of my skin. Grandmont-Rosedale is full of people who count their time in their homes by the decade. Grown children and grandchildren are introduced with pride and joint pain is always a hot topic of conversation. (For the record, fifteen minutes of heat, fifteen minutes of cold, and two aspirins usually does the trick.)

At my first neighborhood community meeting, I faced nine worn, black faces and two white ones. I was easily the youngest person there by thirty years. I suddenly felt foolish, like a kid old enough to know better caught playing pretend. I was introduced and there was a moment of silence before a man with white hair in a worn

UAW jacket said, "Hopefully, she can convince more brave, young people to come and save our neighborhood."

Saving anything was never my intention. I'm not one of those cringeworthy people who claim "saving the city" as their motivation for living here. That attitude ignores the agency and devotion of the people who have already spent their lives making Detroit what it is now. I moved to Minock Park because my dream house, like the kind I wanted to live in when I was a little, was up for sale. I had had enough of the crooked landlords in Corktown and the other central neighborhoods. My intention was to live respectfully, pay my taxes, mow my lawn, and use the power of my vote to make Detroit a better place. You know, like a resident of any place should feel compelled to do.

The Grandmont-Rosedale neighborhoods have weathered Detroit's declines thanks in some part to the Grandmont Rosedale Development Corporation. Many neighborhoods in the city have such corporations, but the GRDC is one of the most successful. It was this organization that restored my charming home. The GRDC maintains the only neighborhood center not funded by the city. They get volunteers together to clean up parks and organize parties. There's even a young professionals group for we few millennials who have started to creep back into the area. But the GRDC's most important mission is simply keeping the five neighborhoods populated. And at that they've been very successful.

Rosedale Park, North Rosedale, Minock Park, Grandmont, and the enigmatically named Grandmont #1 all share borders with some of the hardest-hit neighborhoods in the city of distant gunshots. Because distant and sometimes close by, gunshots are common. But the neighborhoods themselves maintain a parklike charm most of the time. As my friend, a young mother, warned me the week I moved in, "things still happen here." This summer, I was jolted out of sleep when my boyfriend threw his body over mine as five loud pops sounded off on our block. Only a few weeks ago, I was walking my dog in the middle of a weekday when a neighbor urged me to get inside. He had just confronted a pair of masked men prowling the street just a block or two from where we were standing. He had just called into work, faking sick so he could stand watch and make sure everyone on our block was okay. He repeated the Minock Park oath: "Well, you know, we look out for each other here."

I still feel comfortable walking my dog every day. My neighbor street-parks her Mercedes. I hear "it gets better every year" all the time from my neighbors—especially since the streetlights went up on Outer Driver. I like to bring my friends from West Village to see the beautiful Art Deco homes lining streets shaded by huge oak and maple trees. There are plans to turn Grand River from a five-lane road into a walkable boulevard. We have a great independent bookstore, amazing fried food carryout joints, a coffee shop, and soon we'll have a vegan restaurant. It seems like things are on the upswing.

The older residents are still wary, though. Soon, they won't be there to keep the lawns immaculate or mow the few empty lots. The last generation did the work of holding up Grandmont-Rosedale. Is all that love going to be lost when they personally could no longer bend to plant flowers in the medians on Outer Drive? Or when their joints rebelled and they could no longer climb the stairs in their bungalows and instead opted for the one-floor post-war ranch housing of Redford or Warren? I can't imagine the proud older women on my street in nursing homes, much less the suburbs, but that must be in at least some of their futures soon. Who will love this place the way they have?

Grandmont-Rosedale, and especially little Minock Park, isn't super cool. It's not the place to dance and drink the night away. And just like living anywhere in the city, there can be some peril involved. It can seem overwhelming, but the good news is, the burden isn't yours to carry alone. You'll have help. After all, we look out for each other here.

# "No, it's not the East..."

### Sara Jane Boyers

...*h*ad said my husband repeatedly, an East Coast native and a University of Chicago Law School graduate. Yet for years, I, a well-traveled, born-in-Detroit, but almost native Southern Californian, had an admittedly skewed sense of national geography and wasn't so sure about this great American middle. In the last five or so years that view has been radically altered by considerable new experience photographing in my own midwest birth city and in the small specific neighborhood in which I was born: the Bagley district in northwest Detroit.

It was the postwar forties and my family roots were not in Detroit when my father, working there for eight years, married my New York City mother and brought her to Detroit. There, thanks to an almost immediate pregnancy, I was born a little over a year later and then, fifteen months later, so was my brother. When my brother was nine weeks old, our parents packed us into the car and due west we drove to California, where my father, an early advertising madman, was looking for the next opportunity.

Periodically, during the fifties and sixties, my father returned to Detroit to serve on the board of the Penobscot Building, then owned by his former polo-playing friend, a very wealthy Canadian with several other large Detroit properties, the Marine Terminal included, in his portfolio. In Detroit, the board did little but drink, so for my mother, Detroit was not a pleasant topic in our house and I learned little about their years there.

In January 2011, with parents gone and a looming major birthday, I started "DETROIT:DEFINITION," a photographic project on the city of my birth. I wanted to understand this city that identified me, at the very least on those application lines asking my city of birth, and in my response to those many SoCal transplants asking me if I was a "native," to which I would say, "Well, no, I was born in Detroit."

And where did I first go symbolically on that day of my sixty-fifth birthday? To Pinehurst Street, south of Seven Mile and west of Wyoming, where I was born and where my parents lived those first years of their lives together and where grace smiled upon me by giving me the birthday gift of being so graciously received by this neighborhood, opening up my world to those who today live there, the real people of Detroit.

They were standing on the front lawn waiting for me: Veronica and Maurice Faust, the siblings who had inherited their parents' home, my birth home, and in which Veronica presently resided. With them was their older sister, Mary Alma Hammons Faust. I was armed with cameras, as were they. In L.A., I had researched the Fausts a bit, discovering that Maurice, a third-generation auto worker, was an articulate and outspoken representative for the workers in Detroit, known best for a *USA Today* article on options for getting by in a declining Detroit. Mary was a retired teacher and Detroit School Board member and, as the child of UAW workers, a longtime student of the history of the Detroit labor movement. Veronica, my wonderful new friend and sometime host, who sadly died in the spring of 2016, was the one who left, a backup singer out in L.A. who had returned to Detroit to help her aging mother and then worked in the courts until, like so many, her job and opportunities were lost in budget cuts. During our time together, Veronica's life and financial ability to care for her home started to decline as well.

All along Pinehurst and many other blocks of Detroit exist similar stories, and even a vacant house or two where squatters—so far in 2011—were being kept at bay. The population of Detroit today is primarily African American, with a healthy mix of historic and multigenerational Mexican Americans and increasing newer populations of Middle Eastern and Bangladeshi residents. They are auto, steel, and clerical workers; military, business people, and service workers.

Downtown, hip young people have been flowing in, taking advantage of lower rental housing prices and job opportunities in the arts, food, and tech communities. It is downtown that we usually hear about in the national press and it is downtown that is spurring the most development and commerce. Yet it is in the neighborhoods that the true wonder of an historic midwestern city reveals itself through the block-minded, God-fearing people who populate it. These are the neighbors who turn out on the front lawn of a neighbor to celebrate a daughter's prom, captured for Facebook in a slightly queasy drone shot. They are hardworking elders holding on to their property, young people raising families, new community leaders arising from their neighborhoods.

They are active neighbors who gather together to help and support one another; the second gift of my 2011 birthday in Detroit was an invitation from the Faust siblings to attend that first night of the Henry Jolly Memorial Pinehurst Block Club monthly meeting. Named after a recently deceased and well-remembered neighbor, the HJMPBC meets to ensure that an elderly neighbor is made to feel safe; to celebrate another's recent news; to solicit contributions when one neighbor needs financial help to fix a leaky roof; to gather communal funds for the needed snowplow when city services can no longer fund one; and to provide a neighborhood watch. I have been honored to attend not only these meetings, but celebratory events, a Thanksgiving gathering included, and see how the determination, creativity, and resilience of the Pinehurst residents and others are ensuring that even should the city decline further, the block will not. What they radiate is hope and determination.

I have learned that Detroit is all about neighborhood. As I explore further, I continue to be thankful that I lucked out in "my" block and that each time I return to Detroit—eleven visits so far—and drive out to Pinehurst to take my each-visit portrait of my birth home, I am stopped by neighbors passing by, each always with another story of their lives and community.

Now in 2016, there is much change, most of it downtown, but starting to stream outward. Detroit is a beautiful city, with parks and grand avenues throughout, waiting to be refreshed. In the northwest, Sherwood Forest and Palmer Park are holding strong in values and community with lovely homes and even a stellar Frank Lloyd Wright-designed property. Seven Mile is still due for redevelopment, although close by the Avenue of Fashion on Livernois is fast evolving. I stop here as often as I can for April Anderson's amazing carrot cake at Good Cakes and Bakes and love chatting with Eric Vaughn of Eric's I've Been Framed, a terrific art framer and art bookstore concentrating on African American lives. On a frigid fall day when my California metabolism and inadequate preparation found me shivering on Livernois, a fashion shop owner handed me a pair of gloves.

On the Pinehurst block, the Henry Jolly Memorial Pinehurst Block Club now has placed signs at both ends of the block announcing its presence. New friends Eric Jackson and Curtis Liscomb are regularly out on the sidewalk, bringing others outside to chat.

While gentrification has become the other concern in a rapidly changing city, the in-neighborhood revival by current residents and supportive associations is also real and the manner in which they are connecting and holding on is a lesson for us all. This is an important Detroit story and one to which we should listen and honor, wherever we may be.

# What's Really Good?

## *April S.C.*

*I* struggle with describing the greatness of the city I called home. To be completely honest, where I lived wasn't all that great. When I say there is beauty and resilience of my people in the D, I also have to admit to the heartbreak. Heartbreak, uncertainty, and a lot of fear. But fond memories. Many fond memories.

I grew up on Elmira. 'Round the corner from Mackenzie High School. Not too far from Parker Elementary. Right off Plymouth. Next to Ohio. Yeah, right in the hood. Well, at least I didn't live on Dexter and Linwood. But, I've digressed, so lemme get back on track.

I grew up on Elmira, in a neighborhood whose original inhabitants brought to the neighborhood all their best intentions. No matter the race of the person, they all wanted the same thing—a nice, peaceful, quiet, safe neighborhood. I laugh at the safe part, because really, who considers safety unless they have the experience that forces them to juxtapose a safe existence against one that's unsafe. But I know they wanted that as well. 'Cause, during my time on the block, in the eighties, danger was creeping in and the white folks were moving out. Now, reader, you and I can have a two-week-long discussion about this. Yes, two full weeks long. But let's not go there 'cause if we do, I'll get back off track. But, the danger was creeping in, no doubt, and my people, my Elmira people, just hung on, with hope, to be spared. But eventually the danger took residence and it all went downhill from there.

I grew up on Elmira in a neighborhood with an array of folks: seniors, blue collar workers, devoted moms and dads who toiled to make the lives of their families enjoyable no matter the financial circumstances. I grew up in a neighborhood where it seemed that people looked forward to the future, with dreams for their children. But dreams often got hazy in my neighborhood. Hazy, then forgotten.

It wasn't all bad though. Despite watching people get beat up, stuck up, drunk, high, and threatened it was aiight. Despite random shootings and missing that bullet that shattered the glass in my bedroom window, it was aiight. Despite being around people who self-medicated despair with gallons of E & J, Boone's apple wine, Miller High Life, and Smirnoff, it was aiight.

I grew up on Elmira and it was often a storm of uneasiness. But the eye of the storm that I endured in my neighborhood was pleasant. Now this is where the good stuff comes in; the bit of happiness that made life endurable and me durable during my time in the D.

I lived on a block where people depended on each other. We forced community because like anything on the base level of Maslow's Hierarchy of Needs, we needed each other for survival. And not just to get food on the table, but to maintain a level of sanity to make sense of our existence. People in the very heart of a decimated urban area don't have much of what they should have and most never will. But in those areas are microcosms of hope spun from the very real communities we create. Our days may have been full of questions, but there were times we sought to answer them together. And we did this by hanging out on the front porches, and discussing the complexities of life till the street lights came on. We barbecued in the backyards, and we opened our yards to whomever wanted a drink or something to eat. We would laugh and dance and sing and touch happiness in ways wealth and the surety of safety couldn't. We watched each other's children and we fed them when they got hungry, making enough when there never was enough. We lent a couple dollars to our neighbor because we understood that we could spare a bit to share. And why not? That same person would have our back when we needed it. Because that is how all of it worked.

Even though I struggle with describing its greatness, I can't say that the Detroit I knew wasn't great to me. In the midst of all that heartbreak and fear was something that I reference often and wish for today. There was an endearing sense of community right on Elmira. 'Round the corner from Mackenzie High School. Not too far from Tappan Elementary. Right off Plymouth. Next to Ohio. Yeah, right in the hood.

# Bused In and Bused Out: How Judicial Rulings Changed Warrendale

*Lori Tucker-Sullivan*

Growing up, my family lived in Warrendale, a tidy neighborhood where post-war, three-bedroom bungalows lined narrow streets and small businesses served customers on the busy thoroughfares of Warren and Joy Roads. We lived with other families whose adults were most often employed in Detroit's automotive industry. Set on the far west side of Detroit, the neighborhood borders Dearborn on two sides and Dearborn Heights on a third, like a square peninsula jutting out into a sea of suburbia. Though we ventured from the neighborhood on occasion for Tigers games or the auto show downtown, for the most part we conducted our lives within our community. We grocery shopped at the A&P at Evergreen and Paul Avenue, we bought school shoes at the small department stores on Warren, my dad shared Friday afternoon beers with his friends at Chick's or one of the other corner bars, and we dined out on pizza from Stromboli's or chili from the tiny Texas Restaurant.

As one of the few Protestant families, we attended Warrendale Church on Piedmont Street, while most of our friends attended Mass on Saturday afternoons at St. Thomas or Sts. Peter and Paul Catholic churches. I remember my mother preparing Sunday breakfast in our small kitchen, hurrying to get us fed and ready for church, while the radio played country hymns from a radio show in Renfro Valley, Kentucky, a reminder of my parents' southern upbringing, which they left behind when they moved to Detroit in the 1940s.

During the school year, I left home each day, made my way past the well-trimmed lawns of five neighbors' houses, crossed the street with the help of Mrs. Beer, the crossing guard in her blue jacket and bright orange AAA-supplied belt, and walked up the cement steps of the playground to the door of George Washington Carver Elementary School. For the first seven and a half years of my grade school experience, that was my morning routine.

Most of the friends at my Detroit school and in the Warrendale neighborhood were white. We came from Italian, Polish, or Irish families. Some were like me, with parents who had moved to Detroit from the South in search of better-paying jobs. Starting in 1972, federal mandates required that Detroit provide educational experiences that were truly equal for all students. As a result of the Supreme Court's ruling in *Brown v. Board of Education* and subsequent state and federal rulings (one made, ironically, by Judge Stephen Rhodes, who today acts as Detroit Public Schools' Emergency Manager), school systems across the country were forced to integrate their schools. In Detroit, this happened by busing students from the inner city to the west and east sides where the schools had remained segregated.

Warrendale was about as far west as one could go in the city, so on that January day in 1972 as the last half of second grade began, four bright yellow buses pulled up in front of the school and black children I had never met filed in to join us. I quickly became friends with Kim and Adrienne, who attended Mrs. Winton's class with me. I didn't know where they lived, but assumed it was very far away. We seemed to all get along pretty well. Adrienne and I braided each other's hair and talked about listening to the new Jackson 5 song on our Close-n-Play record players. It never occurred to me during that time that Adrienne had to get up a full hour before I did in order to board the bus and ride across town from her old school, Parker Elementary, which was nearly empty after most of its students were divvied up to other schools. It certainly never crossed my mind that she or her parents may have been fearful of what she would encounter when she walked into that school with her two friends. I remember little outcry over this from the parents in my school. I believe, to the extent it was possible at the time, we welcomed the new students.

Together, the black and white kids at Carver came to know each other in limited ways. We learned together, put on plays, sang in the choir, hatched chicks in science class, ate together in the lunchroom, and chose each other as teammates in gym class. As we moved from grade to grade, some students left and others took their place. Adrienne's family moved to Toledo, and I made new friends like Rhonda and Helen. But I never visited their homes, never had sleepovers or pool parties. At 3:00 p.m., our lives were just as segregated as they had been before.

Those in city and state government continued to grapple with busing, wondering if the outcomes were as they had envisioned and often finding them coming up short. At one point, Detroit attempted to implement cross-district busing, taking students into suburban school districts. In 1974 the Supreme Court's *Milliken v. Bradley* ruling halted this plan and stated that any busing scheme had to occur within a district's boundaries. However, in 1976, as I was entering seventh grade, the courts once again decided that present methods were not doing enough to fully desegregate public schools in several U.S. cities, Detroit included.

Seventh grade should have been a time for crushes on boys, further planning my future life with either Hall or Oates, and planning our participation in the summer's many bicentennial celebrations. Major development was happening just south of Warrendale with the opening of Fairlane Town Center, the first mall that we could get to by walking or riding our bikes. It was the first time we regularly ventured into the neighboring suburbs and, though I never really felt out of place, I remember young people looking at me differently when I told them I lived in Detroit, an occurrence that would happen many times through high school and college.

That year was our last in elementary school and we were set to enjoy our time on the top rung of the social ladder. We relished our roles as future teachers and safety guards and no longer played on the dusty gravel playground during lunchtime, but rather sulked in cliquish groups along the chain-link fence behind the softball diamond backstop. As students and teenagers, I don't recall us paying much attention to the plans being made at the school administration office downtown. That was, until letters went home on mimeographed sheets of yellow paper announcing that the seventh grade class would not be attending Carver Elementary School in three weeks' time. We received the letters on January 13, 1976. We would begin attending a new school on January 26.

Many volumes have been written about Detroit, books trying to explain the how and why and when of its near-demise. Writers have studied, analyzed, and even fictionalized this city that my parents moved to in the 1940s and in which I and my siblings grew up in the sixties and seventies. Detroit has always been one of the most segregated urban areas in the country, and white flight from the city has been, along with industry loss, one of the most difficult aspects of Detroit's troubled landscape. Most who have considered Detroit's history chart population decline to times of economic downturn and the racial uprising of 1967. Stagnation, and then loss, of population began as early as the 1940s, but the riots of '67 are often used as the pivotal time from which the population figures of Detroit were unable to recover. In nearly all of the narratives I've read, no one mentions the impact of federally mandated busing as a reason for significant population loss in the city. But in Warrendale, the government's attempts to equal the education playing field changed the neighborhood and the educational experiences of me and my peers completely in just a few weeks' time.

Within hours of those notices going home with our textbooks and homework, parents made phone calls and organized meetings. A gathering was hastily put together, and my parents, whose work kept them from parent-teacher conferences and who spent perhaps twenty minutes at annual open houses, quickly walked down the block and took seats in the school auditorium. Because I had recently produced the school play (in which the protagonist family was equal parts black and white) and knew my way around backstage, I was one of only a few students admitted to the meeting in order to help with curtain-raising and microphone volumes. I watched in surprise and horror as my friends' parents shouted epithets and compared federal judges to Hitler. They challenged parents to stand up to these decisions, to not take them passively as the Jews had done in Germany. Could this really be my neighborhood, my friends' parents, I wondered. No one, neither black nor white, really liked busing, but it was for the most part accepted at our school as long as kids were being bused in. Once we were the ones destined to be sent to far-flung schools, it became a completely different story.

But rather than stay and fight these decisions as they had vowed to do, nearly all my white friends simply left. Their departure showed, ironically, that even with integration of schools, economic disparities still very much existed in Detroit. As soon as decisions were made that impacted those in Warrendale, many white parents sold their houses and moved to the suburbs or enrolled their children in private schools. Several friends suddenly went to live with grandparents or aunts in order to attend schools in neighboring cities like Dearborn or Livonia. Parents who raised their children to be honest now openly lied to school officials about places of residence.

I will never forget leaving Carver Elementary School on that last day shortly after Christmas break. We seventh-graders no longer felt special. Instead, we felt used and afraid. For the first time, I realized what Adrienne and Kim had felt five years before. On January 26, instead of skipping south through the snow, I trudged to the north end of my block to await a bus that would take me to Brooks Middle School some seven miles away. We traveled with eighth graders who had already started classes at Ruddiman, the junior high school that Warrendale kids attended. There were several older kids I didn't recognize waiting at the bus stop. The drive was rowdy and I felt carsick and intimidated by the kids I didn't know. For the first several hours of class that day we were corralled into the large gymnasium, at first remaining together, grouped by the school from which we came. Though I'm sure not the intended plan, we ended up with mostly white kids on one side, and African American kids on the other. Eventually, we were moved into new homeroom classes with strangers. It was not just the kids from my neighborhood that were bused to Brooks. Instead, there were students from throughout the city that were brought together in this educational melting-pot experiment.

I never adjusted to life at Brooks. When I recall it, I see gray, crowded hallways and walls covered in institutional, tan-colored tile. The choir room had a distinct odor that I can still conjure today, a sour mustiness that permeated the room. I had hoped to continue playing cello in the orchestra, but the teacher was no longer interested in teaching and, instead, let us play board games every day. I never made friends other than the few that came with me from Carver. And there were only a few of those students remaining. By the second year, there were fewer still as house after house on our block put up For Sale signs. By the time I reached high school—the point at which busing ended and students went back to attending the school in their neighborhood—I could identify about fifteen classmates who had attended Carver with me. By the time I graduated and Detroit's situation declined even further, that number was four: four students that lived with me in Warrendale. By comparison, my late husband once sat with his yearbook and pointed out thirty-seven students in his suburban high school graduating class that he had known since he was six years old. Overnight, it seemed, I lost nearly all of my friends. I watched from my front porch as they packed up U-Haul trucks and left for good, or drove off to a private school each morning.

I look back now and realize that I truly disliked my middle-school experience.

Granted, middle school is fraught for most teens. But my experience at Brooks was, in nearly every way, an unhappy one. And I truly believe that court-mandated busing is to blame. No one seemed to feel settled or content. Fights broke out regularly, I was mugged in the hallway once, and my locker was broken in to multiple times. It wasn't just that the school was unsafe, but that all of us, black and white, simply disliked being there, disliked being a part of someone else's grand experiment. I have only vague memories of a few teachers and one or two classes. It was not a place of learning, but was instead a place of fear and frustration. Bus rides were even worse, with fights, more petty thefts, and a sense of disregard that comes from having no faith in a system that had failed us.

Most now agree that mandated busing was not successful. I never knew what kind of experiences Adrienne or Kim had at their old elementary school, or whether the conditions were so deplorable that the jolt to their system caused by sending them to Carver was worthwhile. It still bothers me that I never realized the fear they most likely experienced at an even younger age than I did; how unsettled they must have felt, how they likely silently grieved for their old school. By the time I graduated high school, when my friends and I were walking or driving to school, I had a fairly integrated group of friends. But we did that, not a federal judge with a bus. Some things can't be made better, even with good intentions.

And forty years after my busing experience, Detroit schools still struggle with problems that can be traced directly to decisions made when I was a student. In a recent speech, Mayor Mike Duggan pointed out that 27,000 students each day leave Detroit and are driven to schools of choice in the suburbs. So, though they're no longer fleeing the city permanently as my friends' families did, they flee it temporarily each day. And while politicians and judges at the state and federal level continue to debate what is best for students, those young people continue to feel, as I did, like pawns in a rigged game.

Though I spent most of my post-college life in Ann Arbor, I now live in Detroit again, having returned last year after my husband passed away. I chose to embark on a new life experience in a city that is also, in many ways, starting anew. Because I am on my own, I chose to live in a condominium, not a house, so moving back to Warrendale wasn't really an option. I have visited several times since my return to the city to shop at the Middle Eastern markets and check out the neighborhood community garden. The demographics have changed in a positive way, and diverse neighbors now gather to get the best Friday night fish fry at Chick's Bar on Warren, and sample pierogi at one of the remaining Polish restaurants. I recently took my teenage daughter to Fairlane and showed her where I had my first job and where her father and I met. I also drove past Carver Elementary School—the teachers that taught me are now long retired, some even passed on. I parked along my street and watched a beautiful group of children, white, black, Arab, and Hispanic, playing on that gravel playground. I hope they love their life in Warrendale and I hope that their middle-school experience will be better than my own.

# Warrendale, a Chance Medley with Lines from "Brother of Leaving"

## Cal Freeman

The Warrendale neighborhood sits on the far west side of the city of Detroit. Historically it was a Polish Catholic neighborhood with St. Peter and Paul Parish anchoring the community on the north side of Warren Avenue and St. Thomas Aquinas Parish anchoring the community to the south. Both of these churches, where the cops, firemen, and water department workers who once populated the neighborhood sent their sons and daughters to school, have closed now. These city workers whose lawns were immaculate, who would work *metal claws / beneath weed roots to upend useless / plants or plants for which they saw no use,* who would drink beer with VO Canadian Whisky back at Nick's on Warren or at the Tipperary Pub on the Southfield Freeway service drive, who would coach their sons' baseball teams and dream of a day when their progeny would go pro and lift them from their working-class existences (to my knowledge there has never been a professional athlete to hail from Warrendale) have all moved out to remote suburbs like Canton and Fenton. The Tipperary Pub has closed its doors. The countertops in the bathroom at Nick's are routinely coated in a layer of Vaseline so the cretins who sneak in the can to do blow might be deterred.

There are perils involved in writing about a place like Warrendale, my childhood neighborhood in west Detroit and the topic of my first book of poems, *Brother of Leaving*. Nostalgia is a temptation. I'm sure I also open myself up to the charge of engaging in "ruin porn," a banal and malleable term seemingly applicable to anyone who chooses to write about or photograph Detroit in a way that doesn't praise the creative class and suggest that small start-up capitalism will save us.

To say the neighborhood is empty would be both classist and racist. To describe the state of my childhood home would be pathetic or "pornographic."

I still live within two miles of where I grew up, and a strange function of seeing these poems in print is how the reality of any place disappears beneath the words we heap upon it. The poem, "How to Enter a Bank-Owned Home," begins with the line, *I wasn't born in the house of pathos,* then proceeds to give the address of my childhood home. The cover of the book features a shot of the abandoned Tipperary Pub courtesy of my friend and bandmate, Matt Balcer. Trees of heaven obscure the front of the erstwhile pub. "MASHR" has tagged the building with pale blue aerosol paint. There is beauty in the sloppy repetition of that inscrutable name. We can't be nostalgic for this pub where we got our first paying gig because the conditions that created that idyllic, at least in my mind, working-class neighborhood also necessitated this battered and impoverished one.

*volunteer tree, sucker, // this, a tree of heaven; / cavities in rotten wood, // ailanthus altissima, Rhus / succedanea, stinking // sumac, ghetto / weed, naming // one requisite for destruction.*

The ailanthus altissima will rise wherever they are not weeded. Prolific as nuclear families, they will throw up suckers even after their parent trees are killed. Their project is one of sprawl and reclamation.

*A car called Nova announces its absence in viscosity on macadam. Pheasants in the poverty grass / and poverty's antecedents gritting teeth. // A threnody of unsprayed cats... // I pick huckleberries like a sparrow.* In a prose poem from her first collection, *allegiance,* titled, "You Can't Remove the City," Detroit-born poet francine j. harris (who was kind enough to blurb my book) cautions, "don't dare make this a junkyard, where the teeth empty out refrigerator motors."

In *Living in the End Times,* Slavoj Žižek attempts to explain the romance we attach to decamped urban spaces like this: "As Lacan pointed out, this is the fundamental subjective position of fantasy: to be reduced to a gaze observing the world in the condition of the subject's non-existence...'The world without us' is thus fantasy at its purest: witnessing the Earth itself regaining its pre-castrated state of innocence." Of course there was never any innocence to regain.

*Blue tarp over shingle rot, // mossed and scabrous, saplings / growing in the gutter, / the streetlights dark throughout the night.*

We are often told in writing workshops that in order to evoke place, we must learn the names of things and employ them, that if we properly set down the names of towns, landscapes, and plants, we'll capture the place we're writing about that much more fully for our reader. This is Cartesian grammar at its finest, and it is false. Our words will never achieve that sort of presence, no matter how pointed they are. The poet and novelist Ben Lerner writes of "the tragic interchangeability of nouns." Place is the cadence declarative syntax makes, and it will accept any name we might apply and gladly die beneath it.

*In the spume of an uncapped hydrant, / a setting. / In each setting, a sprawling / disjointed list.*

For the last decade or so, the U.S. Department of State has been relocating Iraqi refugees to this West Warren Avenue corridor. *West Detroit / is no believable setting, / but a warren slopes away / from Warren Avenue.* War sends them here the way another war once necessitated a Polish ethnic enclave in Warrendale, the way that structural and amorphous war against black America sends whites sprawling into distant suburbs like a herd of stinking sumacs. The Iraqis are subjected to the panoply of slurs that comprise our native tongue, and *I have been writing letters in the worn-out lexicon of bigots.* Trees of heaven look down upon my childhood home and say:

*You are / the murderous fear in all of us / that inflicts harm in order to be free / of harm.*

# Our Bungalow on Braile

*Ian Thibodeau*

More than anything, my dad talks about the trees. How branches reached up and intertwined over the street to block out the sun. Turned the street into a tunnel. You couldn't see the sky. Same thing on every block he and his four younger brothers would have walked. Trees taller than all the Warrendale bungalows. Shelter, and judging by my dad's affinity for air conditioning, shade. Reprieve for the working class.

There aren't a whole lot of trees on Braile Street anymore.

My grandparents moved off the block in 1996. They lived in the same house, a three-bedroom, one-bathroom, 1920s brick homestead, for twenty-nine years. Raised five kids there. Watched when their last few boys went to a private high school in Dearborn and had trouble getting friends to come over. That was the eighties, prime scoffing time. Watched those kids raise kids of their own, and watched several of those babies play on the front porch. Hosted holidays. That's where we went for the first bit of my life. Papa and Sitty's. My Sitty (Lebanese for grandmother) had a fabulous rose garden in the back of the house. She had tomatoes where the swing set used to be. Her trick was planting them against the brick that held heat from the afternoon sun. She worked a couple different jobs, one of which had her selling Tigers merchandise outside the old stadium the year they won the pennant. In the neighborhood, she coached girls' basketball at Saints Peter and Paul, the Catholic grade school a mile down Sawyer that her five boys went to. One of my uncle's fondest memories is the time he got to officiate one of her games. He gave his mother a technical and threw her out. She was—still is—a little loud.

Sitty says she hasn't seen the house in a decade. And while none of us have ever known her to be very emotional (Mike, the middle child, once asked, incredulously, "You made the Rock cry?!" when he heard she'd read a column I wrote about my grandfather in college), it might be too hard for her to see that the house she and her husband bought and filled together, spent most of their lives in, now has a blue tarp on the roof over the bedroom, plywood over a few windows. That it may or may not be occupied depending on when the last time you drove past it was and, though it's hard to tell because the most recent occupants put up a curtain in the front window, depending on whether or not the ghost light is on in one of the back bedrooms. The brothers, like a lot of people born in Detroit between 1955 and 1980, more or less unconsciously mark some bit of happiness, comfort, or success, based, again more or less involuntarily, on their distance from Detroit. From where they grew up. Of the five, only one lives less than five miles from his childhood home. Sitty lives seven miles away in Garden City. And she doesn't plant roses anymore. My grandfather died in 2015, but Alzheimer's, like the decay that ripped open the tunnel of trees on Braile, started poking holes in his mind sometime around 2009.

The rest of us still have the memories, though.

I know less than twenty years ago there used to be more than just one house on the block where grandmothers would have watched silently, smirking, as their grandbabies ran around the front yard like mad men, children possessed, kids whose mothers didn't cut the Kool-Aid and let them have a couple Popsicles after dinner too. Hopped up on sugar and innocence. Making their matriarchs holler when they got too close to the street or raised that Little Tykes golf club back, back, back to bring it down on their sisters' skulls. (Firstnamemiddlenamelastname) don't you dare! Get your ass over here.

And before that, when those grandmothers were mothers, they stayed up late waiting for their babies to come home. The babies Sitty would discretely sniff for signs of smoke or booze even though she was a chimney, probably had a Winston hanging off her lip, and probably couldn't smell shit, but got her close enough to watch their eyes. That's what teenagers don't get. It's not the smell, the one you try in a last-ditch effort to mask with peanut butter or gum, that does you in. It's how big your eyes get when mama bear walks into the kitchen while you're pounding chips and gulping glasses of water. It's how long it takes you to get your shoes off. The babies who sometimes got to borrow the Ford Torino station wagon, but mostly had to bum rides. The babies who were two for five in crashing that car. My dad still has the curves and bends and winds of Outer Drive through Rouge Park memorized. We used to get that thing airborne, he says. And I also know each of my uncles had a different point of teenage ingress and egress at that house. Scott used the bathroom window. Tim climbed through the upstairs window. My dad, incapable of lying, probably snuck out through the front door and left a note for my grandparents. Hey, ma. I went over to Brian's house to play euchre. Be home in the morning. Something like that.

The block on the far west side of the city was a block of families, and that still hasn't left Warrendale, because you can't fight design. Someone builds a bunch of bungalows, some (seven) of them might get boarded up, but you're still going to have people on their porches watching their people do what they're going to do. Kids still play in the park. Just a few days ago, three men stood in the driveway next to the old Braile house, and they were *laughing*. I mean really holding their belly and hooting. So there's still joy in Warrendale. Still families. Kids still play in the park and bloated uncles clutch sweating cans of beer next to cheap charcoal barbecues set up behind or between the little brick houses. Or maybe they gather in the park down the road. And kids probably still do stupid shit there, too. And they're going to fight, and they're going to steal from the liquor cabinet. But for some reason doing that when the block was without vacants wasn't *sad* or *typical*. It was funny. Still is funny.

Here's how Warrendale is funny.

Before most of those boys got old enough to drive, they played in Rouge Park just a block away. When I was in grade school, spending most of my time playing video games or with friends playing video games, dad lamented his old block. We had enough kids for two baseball teams, he'd say. Pick-up games. We'd play all day. And they played football when it snowed. Mike blew out his knee during one of those games and one of his brothers pushed it back into place, they say. Legendary. Down Spinoza, there's a hill they'd run toboggans on. They all learned to drive stick shift on the steep road nearby. Dad calls the road Derby Hill. They skated on the Rouge and sometimes they fell in. At some point in our legend, Mike and his friends once nabbed a bottle of something from one of their parents' liquor cabinets. Sitty remembers it was whiskey. Mike sprinted home from the banks of the Rouge, really tore ass, to pound on the front door. Something's wrong with Murphy, he told Sitty. I don't know, Ma, he fell in the river. Murphy was passed out drunk by the river. Sitty delivered him to his parents and let Mike have it when *she* got him home. Not sure if they ever told Papa, cause then he would've got it twice. And Tim more than once got tailed home by the neighborhood bullies for having said this or that at the park. He waited in the homestead, under the watchful eye of his father, for the kids to come knocking. When they did, at least one time, Tim came out swinging, pushing the screen door open, connecting, and pulling it closed before the kid could hit him back. Papa made Tim step outside, and then the kid got him. Tim became the fastest runner in the family. Went to Eastern Michigan on a track scholarship. Came home after two semesters and started an apprenticeship as an electrician.

I know the 1967 riots broke out the summer my grandparents moved into the house on Braile, having had three sons in four years in a small house in the Barton-McFarland neighborhood they grew up in. Almost exactly two years later, Armstrong landed on the moon and Papa let the neighbor tell him how it was a conspiracy. They had two more kids. They went to church, even though they might have been one of the only non-Polish families in the neighborhood. Weird mix they were. Half Lebanese, and Papa brought along some Native American and Scottish blood to top things off, so goes the legend. Nearly every one of my uncles' friends' last names ended in *ski*.

My dad had a paper route delivering the *Detroit News*. On Sundays, he made pit stops (plural) at the Sun Rise Bakery on the corner of Warren and Fielding for chocolate milk and chocolate donuts. When his younger brother, Chris, got a route a few years later, he'd toss the ads from the Sunday paper onto the roof of that bakery because it made the papers lighter. The youngest brother, Scott, got a route, too, but he didn't deliver from his bike, didn't have to tow a wagon. Papa woke up early to drive Scott's route with him in the passenger seat. Sitty avoided Warren Avenue on Saturdays—too busy—but frequented the Kresge's Five and Dime on Joy or the Woolworth's on Warren. Polish meat markets, she says, were everywhere if you went past Southfield, and Mike once lit half the park on fire after Chris handed him a book of matches, stood him next to a pile of dried-out grass clippings, and walked away. The cops brought him home that night. They had high school graduation parties in the backyard, and the garage until very, very recently, permanently leaned to the right, and I spent the night on the couch in that living room the night my little sister was born.

Everything that made my family is in that house—came from that neighborhood.

A week after Easter in 1996, Sitty noticed a car circling the block. Rowdy people —black and white—started moving to the block, she said, but it wasn't bad yet. Her friend, Doris, was on her way to the bank and had stopped over to see if Sitty needed anything. We thought maybe the car needed directions, Sitty said. The men stopped in front of the house. Doris told Sitty to go see what they wanted. Before she said a word, one of the guys pointed a gun at her. He got out of the car, ran up the porch and stole Doris's cash-filled purse. They took off.

We're going, Papa declared that night. The house sold by the summer.

They'd give anything to go back, I think. You can't so fondly remember a place or a time without at least some part of you longing to return. Wishing time travel was real. Uncles drive by the place and later tell of how horrible the house looks. I disagree. The whole block is overgrown. The street's cracked. It's hard to tell which shops on Warren are open, which are closed. The Burger King my parents worked at through high school (my dad used to tell a story of how he saved my mom from a pistol-toting robber. Found out later my mom dealt with the robber herself. Dad was in the back manning the fryer) recently got a nice renovation. The grocery store next door is vacant. Someone cuts the grass on the old baseball field around the corner; the backstop is still there, but there weren't any kids whipping through the field. Down the hill, someone's cut a path through the brush to a small basketball court where a group played pickup on a Saturday in July. Through the midsummer growth, you can make out the bank of the route my uncle took me for walks on when we had family parties at the house. The park at Joy and Spinoza has new colorful playground equipment, and grown men fly model planes in the field. On the route my dad would have walked to school, three boys, maybe fourteen or fifteen years old, sit twiddling their phones on the porch of a burned-out house. One of them is rolling a joint. They don't look up as I drive past. Around the block, a group of boys plays basketball in the street. One waves, they move aside to let me through. Pay me no mind. A woman sits on the porch. Two men sit on the porch. A woman lounges on the porch. Two chairs sit empty on the porch of my grandparents' old house.

And still the sun beats down on the beaten down block that the trees try so hard to protect.

# Plymouth Rock Landed on Me

### *Lhea J. Love*

Things aren't perfect
in the hood

there are more abandoned
houses than bodied homes
there are more squatters
than payers

and that woman asking
for spare change

is a friend of mine.

# Bagley

*Barbara Stewart Thomas*

*I* grew up on the northwest side of Detroit in the fifties and sixties in the Bagley neighborhood. I don't remember anyone calling it that back then—Bagley was just the name of my school. We moved there when I was four. Before that, we lived not very far away, in a two-flat on Stoepel, near Curtis. My aunt, uncle, and cousin lived upstairs; we lived downstairs—my parents, older brother, and grandparents all in a three-bedroom flat. My family needed four bedrooms so we moved to the house on Cherrylawn near Six Mile (McNichols, as it was formally called), which looked, literally, like a castle to me.

The houses on my block all had different exteriors, but the interiors of most were identical. Our house was built in 1937. There was a small hallway when you entered through the front door. My cousin painted a mural on the walls when I was a little girl. I have visited the house twice since we moved out—1988 and 2013—and the mural was still there.

The living room had a bay window, a fireplace (I never saw a fire in it), nice furniture, and a piano. The room was only used for company, except for me practicing the piano. Across the hall was a small den. It had built-in wooden bookcases, a TV that only sometimes worked, and a sofa bed. It was mostly my grandfather's room. I did, however, find many interesting old books which had belonged to my older cousin on those bookshelves. One time, my grandfather fell asleep there and dropped his cigarette into the sofa. Luckily, I smelled the smoke and the house didn't burn down.

Down the hall was the "rumpus room." My mother turned the dining room into a family room. This was the most used room in the house. We had an RCA blonde wood cabinet, black-and-white TV, two matching sofas, a couple of end tables, and a bar cabinet for company. We ate dinner on TV tables on most nights, but never on Fridays. There was a screened-in back porch where we often ate dinner in the summer. When it was really hot, I would sleep on the cot out there.

Next was the breakfast room. It also had a small bay window, a plaster ceiling with intricate moldings, and a butler's pantry. That was where we ate breakfast, sometimes lunch, and the Friday night *Shabbas* dinners my grandmother spent all day in the kitchen cooking. The small kitchen through the archway was very basic.

There was a staircase to the basement. On the landing was a grim half-bath—strictly utilitarian. The finished basement was a great place to play as a kid and to have parties as a teenager. There was a wet bar, though I only remember it being used once for a big party. The rec room had a fake fireplace, my grandmother's sewing machine, an old record player and a stack of seventy-eights. This is where the old couches, tables, and lamps ended up. There was also a laundry room with a gas burner, a cellar, and a furnace room.

There were four bedrooms, two bathrooms, and a cedar closet upstairs. My brother's room had a small, unenclosed porch. After my brother left home, I moved into his room. It was larger than my original room and had one of the two phone jacks. The other was in my parents' room. One phone was shared between the two rooms.

The master bedroom and my grandparents' room formed a "Jack and Jill Suite" —that's two bedrooms with a bathroom in between. But there was a dresser against the bathroom door in my grandparents' room, so that bathroom was strictly for my parents. The rest of us used the bathroom in the hall, which had a built-in, tiled, mirrored vanity, separate from the sink.

Our street stopped at Marygrove College, or so it seemed to me then. It was a huge, mysterious presence to me as a child. Online real estate sites say that our house is in a subdivision called "Marygrove Homes Park." Marygrove College was opened in 1927, ten years before our house was built, so it was likely a catalyst for residential development. My father used to say that where we lived had been "out in the country" when he was a boy.

Growing up near Six Mile between Wyoming and Livernois was great fun. There were many stores and I can remember quite a few of them. The best thing was, as kids, we could walk or ride our bikes there. One block west was Herman's Market, where I bought candy and comics. It was a small shop, and Herman was a kindly old man. My grandmother often sent me there to pick up things she ordered from the kosher butcher inside the shop. I remember the chickens with their feet still attached that she would buy for Friday night *Shabbas* dinners.

Going east toward Livernois was much more interesting. There was Nino's, a beauty shop, and Lou's Finer Delicatessen where I would get a Coke and share a plate of fries with my best friend on my block. Lou's is still there. Then Weinger's, a grocery store that was larger and more brightly lit than Herman's, and the bagel factory where my parents sent me for fresh, hot bagels on Sunday mornings. Further down Six Mile was the holy grail: one block alone had a Neisner's dime store, a Sanders, and a Winkelman's. Once a week, my mom would pick me up from school at lunchtime and take me to lunch at Sanders. There was time to stop in the dime store and later, when I was older, we would look at clothes in Winkleman's. On Livernois itself was the Varsity Theatre. There were three neighborhood movie theaters in the area, but the Varsity was the only one within walking distance. It wasn't as nice as the Royal or the Mercury—and was, in fact rather seedy—but it had Saturday matinees for kids.

More exciting than Six Mile was the Avenue of Fashion starting on Livernois and Seven Mile. I would take the bus or even walk in nice weather. I would often stop at the Sherwood Forest branch library on the way home. During my teenage years, we used to hang out at the big Kresge's on the corner of Livernois and Seven Mile. I would get a hot dog and cherry Coke at the lunch counter. If I went with my mom, we would meet my aunt at Billy's Deli. My uncle and aunt owned a shoe store on that block.

If I took the bus, I would have to transfer at Palmer Park, which was the center of outdoor activity for the surrounding neighborhoods—Palmer Woods, Sherwood Forest, the University District, and mine. There was an ice-skating rink in the winter and when I was a very little kid, a wading pool that was later closed because of the polio scare. My grandparents would go to Palmer Park too to meet their old friends and play cards. It was a place for all ages.

I last visited my old neighborhood in 2013. There were a few boarded-up houses, but nothing like you see in other parts of the city. These are solid, middle-class brick homes that might need some fixing up, but have stood the test of time.

Bagley doesn't have the grandeur that Sherwood Forest or Palmer Woods have, nor the cachet of the University District. It never did, but they are houses for people to love and to raise their families. The saddest part of the neighborhood is the state of its main commercial street, Six Mile. There are too many run-down, boarded-up stores. There is some hope coming from the organization called Live6 (Livernois and 6 Mile) and the efforts of Marygrove College and University of Detroit Mercy to bring it back. There have been some great successes with bringing back the Avenue of Fashion and I am hopeful the same thing can happen with the streets I knew so well as a child and teenager.

# Palmer Park:
## A Glorious Crossroad for Nature, Recreation, Creativity, Community, and More
### Barbara Barefield

My first home in Detroit, as a New York transplant and University of Michigan art school graduate, was on Whitmore Street, in one of the elegant apartments in the Palmer Park Historic Apartment District. Surrounded by architecture in eclectic styles from Tudor to Art Deco to Spanish, I was in heaven. Then I discovered the park across the street.

Treasured as a public park for some 125 years, Palmer Park stirs magical memories from the depths of childhood and beyond. Elders who had lived in the area recalled splashing in the fountain, cart and pony rides, ice skating and sipping hot chocolate at the pavilion, ballgames, learning to swim in the pool, picnics with family, campouts, a log cabin with antiques and old-fashioned furniture…the list goes on and on for so many who hold dear to their hearts this 296-acre corner of primeval forest and fields at the northwest corner of Woodward and Merrill Plaisance, just north of McNichols. A bucolic retreat from urban life and day-to-day chores, it was a place to relax, be close to nature, play a sport, grill a favorite recipe.

When I moved to Palmer Park in the mid-1970s, there were art fairs, outdoor concerts, and tennis courts lit up past sunset in the summer. However, by the time I brought my young children to the park to feed the ducks and play on the swings at the end of the 1980s, the park was not quite the paradise it had been in the first part of the century.

In the early part of the twenty-first century, as the city of Detroit's ability to maintain the park decreased, the park deteriorated further. The woods were neglected; a pyramid of trash could be found in one area, and litter throughout. Crime, drugs, and prostitution, as well as neglect of its assets, deterred many from spending time in the park.

In 2009, a group of community members, business owners, and representatives of the city came together to plan the Palmer Park Green Art Fair in hopes of setting seeds to revitalize the park. We worked cleaning Lake Frances and the area surrounding it—dredging the lake, scrubbing the duck poop from the sidewalk, and picking up piles of trash. On June 28, we presented a festival showcasing artists, green environmental advocates, and community organizations with non-stop music at three locations. I designed my first poster for Palmer Park, met some of the other volunteers who would go on to found People for Palmer Park, and fell in love with the park.

By the next week, the pond was filled with dirty diapers, trash was flying around, and garbage containers were few and overflowing. I knew I was not the only one who felt like crying, but had to place Palmer Park on the back burner.

The following summer, a viral battle call emanated from the Palmer Park tennis players. Lee King, who had played on the courts since childhood, sent out a cry (and press release): "You cannot close our tennis courts!" In response to a threat from the economically distressed city government that the park might be closed, Lee helped to organize a rally, attracting some 150 park supporters.

This outpouring may have been the reason the city did not close the park, but a core group of those who attended the rally—including Lee King, Rochelle Lento, Helen Broughton, Lori Heinz, Alicia Biggers, Kim Fracassa, Dan Scarsella, and others—decided that a long-term strategy and committed group must be formed to transform the park in a sustainable manner. They began to meet and form People for Palmer Park (PFPP). The following year it became a 501(c)(3) nonprofit organization and the official "Adopt-a-Park" partner with the city of Detroit.

The challenge to transform the park was approached from numerous angles to both clean and beautify the park, present programs and events that would bring people into the park, and encourage volunteerism from all segments of the community. There was cleaning (including pulling a shopping cart out of the pond), planting, much hard work, but also a special exhilaration when you sense change.

With a shoestring budget and an all-volunteer board, People for Palmer Park members worked to create a plan to revitalize the park—and develop a camaraderie that crossed racial, economic, and neighborhood barriers. The park became a magnet and vortex for developing friendships, creativity and community building.

In 2011, there were few organized recreational activities at the park, so Lee King, our tennis queen, started the PFPP Tennis Academy. From a handful the first season, it has grown to a five-day-a-week program with some 100 students of all ages. Working with other groups, such as Coach Garrett Street's Legends Baseball League, the baseball diamond was repaired and Little League games returned to the park after a fifteen-year absence. Now a youth football and cheerleading group developed through the Detroit Police Athletic League is also using Palmer Park.

The park is once again brimming with activities, including a new playground and the third year of a community garden built with support from Home Depot.

Free yoga classes on Saturday mornings now attract forty to sixty people each weekend (shavasana under the sun with birds singing has never been so glorious!). Similarly, on Tuesday evenings, free t'ai-chi classes inspire good health and energy.

Popular weekly bike rides include some 200 cyclists of all ages on Thursday evenings. Walking groups—with a devoted following—meet three times a week.

The park is now filled with cyclists, walkers, runners, and people playing volleyball or throwing horseshoes. Soon the dilapidated Chess Row area will be filled with young chess champions as PFPP is working with Sit On It Detroit to rebuild the chess tables in Palmer Park. In another corner of the park by the Splash Park, a Little Detroit Free Library encourages reading and literacy by offering free books for all through a "take a book, leave a book" sharing process.

The city of Detroit has relocated the Mounted Police Headquarters back to Palmer Park, and the excitement of feeding apples and carrots to the beautiful horses, as well as seeing them proudly march through the park and neighborhoods, are joyful experiences.

Birds, deer, raccoon, fish, and an array of other creatures live in Palmer Park—as well as the mythical, magical, miniature flying Aziza, who live in the Aziza Village in the woods, protecting the trees and nature. Children in PFPP's Magic of Art in Palmer Park program crafted tiny doors for these angels from Africa and sometimes the flutter of their wings or their silhouettes can be detected in the enchanted forest between the Splash Park and Mounted Police Station. The thrill of children running and exploring the woods as they search for the small doors and Aziza makes my heart jump. The woods should be teeming with curious humans, but it is usually empty.

In 2012, one of the first headlines to hit the news about PFPP was our new apple orchards—we planted about 800 trees. We could not imagine a controversy about planting trees in a park, but fears abounded at first. Those concerns have now diminished, and while the orchards are a huge amount of work to maintain, PFPP hopes to harvest apples for our annual HarvestFest and collaborate with Motor City Brewing Works to have a signature cider in the future that will help to raise funds for the park.

The park is coming alive after many decades of neglect, and although there is much to restore, repair, or rebuild—like the Merrill Fountain, the tennis courts, the Log Cabin, and a new Pavillion—we are well on a path of creating a special gathering place "for the good of everyone," as Senator Palmer wished when he deeded his land to the city and Detroit citizens.

The journey continues, my love for the park and my fellow People for Palmer Parkers grows, and perhaps one day I will have grandchildren who will feed the horses or ducks with me and I can tell them, "I remember when the cabin was padlocked, the trails through the woods were filled with debris, the fountain was covered with weeds and graffiti—and now look at this magnificent park!"

# Biking University District

## John G. Rodwan, Jr.

*– After "Jogging Sherwood Forest" by Murray Jackson*

Yes, students pass through every day.
Along with repairmen's vans, people walking
dogs, kids fooling as light flits between leaves
on sidewalks, roads, and me.

Bluebirds aim to impose their wills
as sparrow minions skitter from one
chain-link fence perch to the next.

Serene mourning doves wing whistle,
cardinals flash crimson,
proud robins screech and forage.

Driver-disregarded stop signs create risks
at each corner of the neat grid.

Pedaling steadily forward on Saturday morning
to the Senator's green preserve—
Palmer Park.

Casually discarded Better Made potato chip
bags and fast food remains feed the birds,
chipmunks and opossums, even.

Yes, All Saints can be found on Seven Mile but
Mercy's a mile away.

*– Originally published in* San Pedro River Review, *Fall 2013*

# Sherwood Forest

## Gail Rodwan

*E*very neighborhood is special if you live there. It may be special in a good way or a bad way, in a way you hardly ever think about or in a way you think about every day, but special nonetheless because it is the place against which you measure every other place you go in life and every person you meet outside the neighborhood.

The author Edna Ferber wrote in her prize-winning novel *So Big* that the world is made up of two kinds of people: emeralds and wheat. Emeralds are the people who create and appreciate beauty. Wheat are those who create and appreciate the necessities of life. The emerald/wheat metaphor can be applied to places as well as people, and, when it is applied to places, Detroit and the neighborhoods that comprise it are surely wheat. Detroit is a city that works hard, gets tired, gets dirty, gets defeated, and picks itself up every day and keeps going with a tenacity that amazes anyone who is paying attention. It is full of beauty, but it is not a beautiful city. It is full of extraordinary things, but it is not an extraordinary city in the ways New York, Paris, or San Francisco are extraordinary cities. It does not sparkle like an emerald.

Or does it? A few years ago, an aspiring politician famously said with derision that Palmer Woods—a lovely neighborhood that adjoins my own Sherwood Forest neighborhood—was "not a part of Detroit." What he meant was that Palmer Woods is an emerald in a city of wheat and thus, not just atypical, but inauthentic. I have learned that is not true.

For me, a forty-six-year resident of Sherwood Forest who grew up in a nice little college town on the west side of the state, my neighborhood gleams for surface reasons and for reasons that go deep. The historic homes are beautifully built and beautiful to live in. The winding streets are quiet and green with trees. We exchange books at two Little Free Libraries, both of which were lovingly built by one of our own neighbors. We exchange ideas at Livernois cafés and restaurants or on our own stoops and in our own backyards with neighbors of all backgrounds and ages, who appreciate one another as much as anyone we know. We frequent Baker's Keyboard Lounge, a sophisticated jazz club that is said to be one of the world's oldest, with a piano-shaped bar that impresses almost as much as the renowned musicians who have loved playing there over the years. We attend plays and lectures at University of Detroit Mercy and Marygrove College. We take picnics to Palmer Park, a green space that has experienced an unprecedented renaissance in recent years thanks to the hard work and commitment of dedicated neighbors.

Is everything coming up emeralds in Sherwood Forest? Of course not. But no one is surprised when, at our annual meetings every May at a local church, neighbors who have lived in Sherwood Forest for anywhere between one year and fifty years stand up and say, "There is nowhere I would rather be." Isn't that what it means to live in a beautiful place? And I'm not just talking about Sherwood Forest now. I'm talking about Detroit. In this city so dense with wheat, and, yes, crushing adversity as well, emeralds are sprinkled everywhere. Detroiters love their neighborhoods—not just neighborhoods like Sherwood Forest, but all neighborhoods; not just downtown or midtown, but Delray and Brightmoor, too. Look around you, and you will see Detroiters creating beauty in our vibrant street art, lush community gardens, well-used parks, and treasured homes.

# Sing, Shout, "Green Acres is the Place to Be!"

## Maureen McDonald

The lights go out throughout the house. Once a bubbling, convivial party, the crowd hushes and anxiously waits by candlelight as Frank and Karen Hammer scurry around the kitchen pouring bottles of port and claret and bags of almonds into a soup pot. They toss in raisins, cardamom, allspice, and cloves. Then the finale. The pair soaks sugar cubes with a fifth of whiskey and the amazing "Glogg" ignites the night.

Everyone, including me, shouts hooray. With a soup ladle, Karen pours dollops of the thick mixture into coffee cups. Each face lights up with the taste of holiday cheer. People laugh, sing Christmas carols, and swap baby/grandbaby pictures with a taste of friendship and good liquor. I look around the room at friends, neighbors, fellow members of the Green Acres Citizens Patrol, and think: the neighborhood that watches over each other stays together, in duty and in friendship.

Folks protect their neighborhood on rotating schedules every day of the year and celebrate their accomplishments twice a year in winter and summer. Though I moved out of Green Acres Woodward Community a few years ago, I come back for patrol parties. This is the community's gift to itself, for protecting 1,000 families and their real estate investment.

More than 100 members strong, the radio patrol members log 1,098 annual miles and punctuate progress with bountiful potluck parties and victory stories. Vigilant for three consecutive decades, they know the reward. Crime is down, housing prices are over the $100,000 mark according to Curbed Detroit, an online real estate magazine. Even the two streets with the highest crime reports—Sheffield and Gardendale—are increasingly occupied by taxpayers instead of drug dealers. Dozens of young couples, gay and straight, are moving into this comfortably integrated swath of land a half-mile wide and a mile long. Residents say its patrol is one of the largest and most sustainable citizen efforts in the city of Detroit.

"We look out for each other," says Karen Hammer, a member of the radio patrol since 1994 and the former president of the Green Acres Woodward Civic Association, an organization active since the mid-1930s. "This is a warm, wonderful neighborhood with tree-lined streets and beautifully crafted brick homes. We have a responsibility to keep it up."

Over time the residents have beaten back a formidable crime wave, rebounded from recessions and riots, helped shutter a bar that was a hotbed of prostitution and drugs, and stopped Mario Andretti and theater impresario Joe Nederlander from putting a racetrack on the Michigan State Fairgrounds. The lovely shopping strip on Livernois is rebounding with community help. And flowers grow throughout the neighborhood.

To be sure, Green Acres is one of the few neighborhoods where strangers break out in song when residents say where they live, recalling an Eddie Arnold and Zsa Zsa Gabor comedy that ran from 1965 to 1971: *Green Acres is the place to be...*" A community of modest, well-designed homes, it holds the northern corner of a square mile of beautiful houses, mid-sized mansions in Sherwood Forest and magnificent houses in Palmer Woods. The perimeter includes the historic Michigan State Fairgrounds and the elite Woodlawn Cemetery. Street life includes ten lanes on Woodward Avenue and eight lanes on Eight Mile Road. Within fifteen minutes a resident can get to Birmingham to the north and downtown to the south, making it one of the most convenient locations around.

"When you know your neighborhood, you watch out for everyone. You feel like you are part of something that serves the common good," says James A. Ward, a retired Ford Motor Company executive who devotes endless hours coordinating the patrol and its twice-annual celebrations in mid-summer and winter.

The regulars say Jim can be frustrating, with all the requirements he issues patrollers about filling out forms and re-reading the procedures manual. But the team knows their volunteer hours have an impact because of his meticulous organization. There are almost no empty houses; nearly everything is restored after the 2008 mortgage crisis. The lights are back on, lawns mowed and young families are walking baby carriages. Jim and his wife Sheila are benevolent parents and grandparents to a community. The enveloping kindness helps.

Nearby neighborhoods have been ravaged by drugs, disinvestment, and dire times, and Green Acres could have been a casualty. A "once was" kind of place. Much credit goes to an abundance of lawyers, civic activists, and journalists in this small community who took action again and again to protect the community from harm inside and out. I fell in love with this place in the mid-1970s, fresh out of Michigan State University. Swore I'd live here eventually. And did so.

## TWINKLING KIND OF NEIGHBORHOOD

Growing up in the suburbs and forbidden to hang in Detroit as a teenager, I headed straight to the city when I graduated and rented an apartment in Palmer Park, a glorious collection of brick apartment buildings on the border of one of the most beautiful parks in Detroit. A vibrant group of young people took up the mantle of protecting the city some of our elders deserted and made it a blast to build alliances and beautify streets.

I took up riding through the winding, curved streets of Green Acres with my then-boyfriend Charles, a Detroit city planner. He called it a twinkling kind of neighborhood for the golden glow of porch lamps and the fancy frontages that greeted us as we glided by on our three-speed English racers.

Streets have proper names of London lore—Briarcliff, Lichfield, Canterbury, and Piccadilly—as though the Queen herself lights the way with a scepter.

What I found here was illuminating. People were always hosting parties in these charming homes, whether chamber music concerts in the living room, jazz trios in the backyard, or block parties with rock and roll. Lots of mixed-race couples and gay couples who felt welcome here. We'd spend nights listening to great music at Baker's Keyboard Lounge, the oldest jazz club in Detroit, a landmark in Green Acres.

I'd meet loads of journalists, liberal lawyers, schoolteachers, and social workers. In the first decade past the Detroit riot of 1967—when forty-three were killed in a five-day melee, 1,189 injured, and 2,000 buildings destroyed—the cool people moved into Detroit. They wanted a direct say about civil rights and social justice. The city's population stood at 1.5 million people then, but the schools throughout the city were emptying out by forced busing and increased crime. Others fled to cookie-cutter colonials that rose up in the second-ring suburbs of Troy, Dearborn Heights, Harrison Township, and Farmington Hills. Challenges arose for the newcomers.

The late real estate agent, Chris Celinski, a champion of historic preservation, would call it the "rule of five." Couples would move into the neighborhood filled with dreams of raising generations on these tree-lined streets in their gingerbread Tudor houses. Then a child would turn school age and they would leave for communities with higher education ratings. Detroit schools didn't make the grade, he'd say with sorrow. Being childless, I stayed happily ensconced in the city.

Over the years I occupied several dwellings in Green Acres, but the best—the one I stayed fifteen years—was a 1,200-square-foot Irish cottage with a high-pitched roof on Lichfield. The ivy-covered entrance invigorated my soul and charmed all who came to visit. The backyard was a bit dicey. Some loved, some were spooked that I lived behind Woodlawn Cemetery, a forty-four-acre collection of sculpture, personal mausoleums, a small lake, and beautiful plantings just south of Eight Mile and west of Woodward.

The placid marble gardens resonated with the sound of bugles, bagpipes, and drumming that accompanied the red canopy and graveside ceremonies. I'd thread my bicycle by stately mausoleums housing auto barons John and Horace Dodge, retail giant J. L. Hudson, Senator James Couzens, and a host of others. In later years, Detroit councilwoman Kay Everett and civil rights leader Rosa Parks were interred here. One time, I made love on top of a stone sarcophagus with a handsome historian, but that's another story.

Lifelong resident Michael Dallen told me the cemetery and the neighborhood parcel were a joint package that started as swamp land until the developers of Woodlawn Cemetery came along in 1896 when this chunk of land was known as Greenfield Township, a suburb of Detroit. The company sought to create an eternal home for the city's rich and mighty.

The graveyard developers would finance their investment by selling lots west of the cemetery in two subdivisions, Green Acres and Woodward, which joined into one neighborhood in the 1930s. Lot owners then bought plans for kit homes from Sears, Wardway, Aladdin, and Lewis and hired custom builders to make them unique. A big draw was the abundant mass transit—first street cars, then buses—serving the factories of Highland Park and the giant offices in Detroit's New Center. Over 60 percent of the gingerbread brick homes were constructed between 1940 and 1959, with 81.7 percent single-family dwellings, according to the U.S. Census Bureau. Nearly every house had an interesting door welcoming visitors. Garages were tucked in the backyard.

Research on this jewel of a neighborhood is remarkably thin, yet the neighbors are some of the most dynamic people in the city. Friends from Green Acres filled me in.

Dwight and Sandi Kirksey said they moved here in 1973 determined to make a home and helped build a friendlier community. They linked with other young couples who dedicated themselves to the urban dream. The first activity was a recycling newspaper committee. Once a month, Dwight would rent a two-ton dumpster. Residents then read so many different papers daily, the organization could fill a dumpster and haul it away. The cash paid for flats of flowers that the environmental committee planted at all the major corners. But the winds whipping through the streets were increasingly unkind.

"By the mid-1980s the neighborhood began to take a beating," Dwight recalls. "Redlining took over. Even though Sandi and I had professional jobs and excellent credit, we had a hard time getting financing for a remodeling. At a time, people sought to add family rooms, two-car garages and finish their basements they couldn't get the cash. Some of them moved out to the suburbs where financing was readily available."

Rent was pretty cheap in the mid-1980s. For $400 a month, I had a 1,200-square-foot upper flat with a turret in my fabulous neighborhood. I'd graduated to a twelve-speed Raleigh and rode around Green Acres daily. The view was as pleasant as any suburb. Trash was picked up weekly, lawns mowed, and shutters freshly painted. But I got the creeps riding past the Last Chance Bar on the southeast corner of Eight Mile and Woodward. Men would leer at a woman on a bike as if they could toss her into an abandoned storefront and have their way with her.

Periodically, prostitutes haunted the external corners of both Livernois and

Woodward. Customers were bold enough to conduct liaisons in driveways and toss spent condoms and beer cans onto the lawns as though no one would care. Residences were indignant. The economy made things even more onerous.

The city took a brutal downturn in the late 1970s and early 1980s. American cars stopped selling in record numbers. Automakers and their suppliers shuttered plants left and right, leaving some with high-paying jobs and serious addictions to find new sources of income with nefarious industries—the drug racket, burglaries, and car thefts. Crack cocaine, the most addictive drug known to mankind, began turning people into zombies who would steal anything, rob a preacher or a pregnant woman for their habit. Dwight says 130 homes were invaded by burglars in 1986.

Faced with the dilemma of moving en masse or standing tall as a unified citizenry, the people picked up CB radios, forming one of the first patrols in the city of Detroit, led by Dwight's wife Sandi, the first patrol coordinator.

Volunteers would sign up for two- or three-hour shifts and report back to a base station by radio or cell phone; they drive slow enough to record license plate numbers of suspicious cars and they watch well enough to eyeball a set of keys left hanging in the front door. Strict protocols govern actions, whether to shine a light on a pair of lovers necking in the alley or to report a drug deal in progress in Hyde Park, a pocket park at the west end of the neighborhood.

Chatting up the neighbors was fine but interacting with suspected wrongdoers was out of order. No *Hill Street Blues* action allowed. Watch. Report. Watch some more. If they saw a man stopping a suspicious woman on Eight Mile they would write down the license plate number on the log sheet. The cops and prosecutors cooperated. Cars could be impounded when the driver was engaging in illegal solicitation.

With a reduction of home invasions, banishing prostitutes on the corner, residents were emboldened to tackle the biggest breeders of crime: the Last Chance Bar. Around the same time period, they worked with zoning officials, vice cops, and precinct captains to slap ordinances on the bar to restrict illegal activities that metastasized around its parking lot, spreading ill will around the neighborhood. Gabe Glanz, who also owned the Grande Ballroom in the 1960s, took the bar into eventual bankruptcy. The city bought it and bulldozed it, along with 1,000 tiny houses in a blighted neighborhood next to the fairgrounds. People received a pittance, but they got out.

Other neighborhood groups took the lead and forced closures of some of the Woodward strip's flea bag motels where clerks rented rooms by the hour, discount prices if they didn't change the sheets.

"We could breathe again," says Dwight. Within one year of citizens patrolling its streets and shuttering the bar, crime went down to just thirty-nine incidents and kept dropping. Thirty years later, active volunteers maintain their watch even when they aren't assigned. Everyone is a deputized patroller in the ongoing campaign against crime and blight.

## "CAR 54, WHERE ARE YOU?"

When I first donned my official yellow patrol jacket and hooked up the CB radio in my VW Jetta, I thought I'd be cruising into a *Mod Squad* episode, nabbing criminals by their collar and absconding with their drugs. Nope. The James Ward-Twelfth Precinct protocols are clear. If we see a drug deal or a burglary going down, we report it to the base captain who calls it into the police station. Our role is passive observer, not Dirty Harry.

When the patrol group is short-staffed, volunteers call the police direct with emergency situations—from a drunk seen face down in the snow to an angry couple plugging up traffic in both directions by conducting their argument in the middle of a narrow street.

"What fascinates me is the relationship this community has with the police," says Karen Hammer, former president of the neighborhood association and an active member of the radio patrol since the early 1990s. "People feel free to call the police and they are generally responsive. We help them, they help us," she says.

Indeed, Sandi Kirksey recently heard a recent report of a man posing as a Guardian Alarm representative. He rang her neighbor's doorbell, pounded on her door and insisted on entering her house to service the alarm. When she refused, he kicked a hole in her storm door and cursed at her and her husband. She captured a picture of the fake technician on her smart phone and sent it to Sandi, who circulated it to everyone on the patrol roster and the administrators of the Twelvth Precinct. The police continue the search.

Being watchful when off duty was lifesaving a few years back. I was driving to a class I taught at Focus Hope's college prep program when I heard a faint cry for help on a zero-degree day on Lichfield. Had I been playing the radio, I may not have heard her. A lady had slipped and fallen on her ice-covered driveway. She didn't have the strength to lift herself up the porch steps. I stopped my car. Ran to help but she was too big to lift. What now? If I called 911 it could take an hour and frostbite would set in. I ran to a neighbor's home where a couple beefy construction guys were installing a new kitchen. They ran over, lifted her up and escorted her into her house.

Karen Hammer keeps her eyes open for many dilemmas. Her environmental committee targets homes in disrepair and labors to rake leaves, mow lawns, shovel snow, and conduct minor repairs on homes so they look occupied and presentable. Patrollers going slow enough can observe a door jimmied open, a window that could let in burglars. As urban champions throughout the city come to realize, scavengers will come and grab ornate chandeliers, mahogany paneling, or copper piping. Some houses are beyond protection.

"The conservation committee got together, brought picket signs to a city of Detroit meeting at the Northwest Activities Center to get a house condemned and demolished on Lichfield. City officials were dragging their feet. Raccoons took over the property, endangering the toddlers next door," she says. The WDIV news crew reported the protest. Soon, the property was demolished, removing one of the biggest eyesores in the neighborhood. The parents breathed a sigh of relief as their children could play out of doors again.

In a spirit of the late activist and author Jane Jacobs, a resident of New York's Greenwich Village, the Green Acres citizen patrollers, association officers, and environmental committee people believe in walking, cycling, and slow-driving the neighborhoods, stopping to chat with homeowners and learning their stories. Jim would say half the effort is stopping crime from occurring, and that the other half is environmental gravity—people dedicated to staying and building up their neighborhood by removing eyesores, protecting children from harm, and using space to its maximum potential. Conversations are webs that connect and reward.

## THE WHITE ELEPHANT IN THE CORRIDOR

Word spread so fast from house to house, the phone lines almost burned up in 1999. Theater impresario Joe Nederlander was buying a thirty-eight-acre portion of the 162-acre Michigan State Fairgrounds to build a racetrack. The newspapers and television stations were filled with praiseworthy articles about a $200 million development that would include retail, three hotels, and a world-class track. Mario Andretti, racing legend, was trotted out for a press conference on the site, just across the street from Green Acres and upscale Palmer Woods.

Neighbors on both sides of the Eight Mile and Woodward viaduct joined forces in 2000 to thwart the racetrack by forging an ad-hoc group, ICARE. Noise wasn't new. Residents endured eleven days of nonstop bands and carnival riders' squeals during the annual state fair each August with nary a complaint. But NASCAR vehicles would roar weekends from spring to fall, maybe eight or ten events annually. Cars would travel 200 miles an hour with open throttles. Airships could circle overhead towing banners for car dealerships. People would park their cars all over our neighborhood streets to avoid paying parking inside the grounds. The noise and traffic jams would be intolerable, the locals said.

I wrote passionate columns decrying the action for the *Detroit News*. Fabled GM Designer Ed Welburn took a visible role of opposition. Protesters jammed the streets in front of the fairgrounds. Every lawyer with chops joined the effort to file lawsuits to stop the development. Attorney and Palmer Woods resident Eugene Driker led the legal effort to uphold Detroit zoning restrictions against a racetrack on the site. Up against formidable odds, the blessings of state officials, and encouragement from auto enthusiasts around the region, the resistance seemed futile.

"No one thought we could win and we did, thanks to all the people that were mobilized," says Dwight Kirksey, a retired lawyer for the National Labor Relations Board. "We were right in the long run. The city and state would have poured countless dollars into the development. In the next decade, NASCAR has almost gone out of business. We'd be left with an empty hulk that drag racers would frequent on

Friday nights."

By 2010, then-governor Jennifer Granholm shuttered the 160-year-old Michigan State Fairgrounds, leaving an eerie chill over the historic site. The fairgrounds on the northwest corner became Gateway Plaza, opened in 2013, anchored by a Meijer, a Starbucks, and a PNC Bank. This became a magnet for customers, a boost to Green Acres residents who could find shopping close enough to walk or bike. For the developers, the strong sales volumes at these stores made the notion of turning the entire fairgrounds into a mall more viable.

City planners envisioned the remainder of the land used for a town within a town, with hundreds of apartments, senior housing, a Wayne County Community College District location, a pocket park, and dozens of small shops and fast food retail. Earvin "Magic" Johnson, the former basketball hero, announced plans in 2013 to buy and develop the land with partner Joel Ferguson, CEO of Lansing-based Ferguson Development, to make a major mall. But the earth-movers haven't arrived yet.

Big money is happening downtown and Midtown, not on the outskirts of town. Reports of the project being downsized have circulated. Echoes of farm animals and roller coasters blow through the wind with the tumbleweeds. Impassioned residents of Green Acres and neighboring communities submitted elaborate plans to re-wild the fairgrounds with trees, native grasses, a farm and garden education center, and a museum of State Fair artifacts. But birds and blooms don't grow a tax base.

Meanwhile, at the west end of Green Acres, the Livernois strip is getting the best infusion of grant money and retail excitement in decades.


## RETAIL REDUX

As a child, my mother would put me in my best dress and white gloves for a trip to the Avenue of Fashion on Livernois between Eight Mile and Seven Mile Roads, the Rodeo Drive of Detroit in the 1950s and 1960s. Quaint one-story, suburban-style shops flanked a mile of retail activity. A giant B. Siegel department store anchored the strip and Cunningham's squatted on a corner with a large soda fountain. If I stayed quiet through my mother's adventures, I'd get a milk shake.

Stores such as Peck & Peck, Pickwick, Claire Peron, and Hunter's Steak House did a thriving trade. When the Somerset Collection opened in 1969, it cherry-picked some of the best boutiques. Soon, a portion of the residents of the affluent housing of Palmer Woods, Sherwood Forest, and University District moved to sprawling ranch houses in the suburbs, close to the new shopping malls. Newcomers buying historic homes found crushing repair bills, leaving less disposable cash.

In the mid-1970s, Alfred Taubman opened shopping malls in more affluent suburbs of Troy, Dearborn, Novi, and Clinton Township that defined retail shopping. The days of sauntering city streets seemed over for Livernois. Over the years unoccupied buildings came down. Instead, a U-Haul franchise took up a whole city block, and New Prospect Baptist Church's parking lots occupied several boring blocks. Hope for revival simmered for ages, then percolated.

In the last five years, University Commons, a consortium of two higher educational institutions, the University of Detroit Mercy and Marygrove College, sought to improve the Livernois strip in partnership with Detroit. The neighborhood has long benefitted from the enduring presence of two Roman Catholic colleges and the ability to use the resources of the architectural and business students to help market and upgrade homes and businesses.

Sweetening the mix, the University Commons helped score facade improvement grants, offering fifty-fifty matching dollars to eligible property owners. Over 160 LED lights flank the streets and parking lots, making the way walkable again. Simply Casual has a regionwide following for hip clothes and the 1917 American Bistro is one of the best restaurants in northwest Detroit. Kuzzo's Chicken and Waffles even enjoyed a visit from President Obama in 2015. Pop-up shops have hosted artists, fundraisers and community meetings.

Kim Tandy, executive director of University Commons, told *Model D* the whole strip will come alive in coming years as urban living enjoys a renaissance.


## BOUNCE-HUSTLE-BIKE-SOCIALIZE

Anyone who signs up for patrol gets invited to both the annual parties, according Jim Ward, who has a legion of party volunteers who help select a menu, assign volunteers to bring certain dishes, and pay Carol Bell to work her magic on ribs, chicken, and greens. Those with add-on family rooms and finished basements offer to take the winter shift; others with big backyards host a summer bash.

Between the wine in summer and glug in winter, people lubricate their commitment to guarding the neighborhood with the best intentions. They swap stories and swat mosquitoes for endless hours. Sandi Kirksey tells how one volunteer saw a thief hot-wiring a car parked on the street. She took pictures and emailed them to the base captain and to the Twelfth Precinct. The guy was caught in days because his rap sheet was familiar.

"We also send cards and financial gifts for births and deaths of community members and their immediate families. These aren't just volunteers, they are family," Jim says. Both the citizens patrol and the neighborhood association join forces to host a Family Day for residents in June and a jazz concert in September at Hyde Park. The residents of Renfrew host an annual block party with a bounce house and a deejay who teaches young and old how to do the hustle.

On my former block of Litchfield, Sandi and Dwight host an annual caroling party and potluck dinner for friends and neighbors. For thirty consecutive years, frigid cold or icy rain, folks glide up and down the three-block street singing to people in each house with a lit porch light. It weaves a sense of community even if the voices are off key. We're best at "Jingle Bells."

Almost no one who lives here sings, "*Green Acres is the place to be.*" Yet they know it in their heart. Be safe. Be well.

Editor's note:
*Some quotes in this story appeared in a July 2016* Neighborhood News Hub *article on Green Acres Citizen Patrol*

*Closing*

# Detroit: Exodus

### *Will T. Langford IV*

It is heavy, heavy, realllll heavy
and we're back brother
like barbershop crisp high top fades
and kicks

in the barbed bosom
of the city that harbored us
hardened us

and made us shine

with smoke on its skyline
tectonic plate-like shifting pavement
and steel in its breath

We're on the I-75
I'm shotgun in your Chevy.
It is heavy, heavy, reallllll heavy

We're back brother
Like Bob Marley's "Exodus" is on wax
and spinning in reverse
calling us
home
home
is where my heart is buried in a tar

It is heavy, heavy, realllll heavy
like oil sands
sweat glands pouring crude

these rude boys
and American girls

dolls
Addie-kink curls
locked
cocked back and loaded
goaded into entering the
inviting night
of my city's rumbling belly

It is heavy, heavy, realllll heavy
With Coney dogs
and sour straws
we're back for both
back from both coasts
with pea coats and stubble

and it's different
we're older
from here
of here
Detroit bred here
and
fed here

but left here…

We're part of a generation
that must take flight
to fight our
reputation

We *are* the Exodus,
Yes.

and will be the Genesis
of a Detroit built of books
and the bright crooked tooth smiles
of children whose bright future will be no myth, brother
our evolution will be live and televised for those eyes cast askance

live and televised for the fair-weather fans
our winters are too harsh for you
It is cold in the D.
and we're tucked deep southeast in the mitten.

It is fitting then
that your fear what it is we do in the dark.
Hark, my burning lover calls my name

Sip your wine, tourists.
Enjoy your casinos.
We've gone,
but we'll be back.
You've spend enough time gambling
to know you should *always* bet on black.

# Contributors

**Barbara Barefield** has lived in the Palmer Park area since 1975. She is a board member and events chair for People for Palmer Park, a graphic designer, photographer, and ceramic sculptor. She is a Knight Foundation Arts Challenge winner for her photography and book project, *JazzSpace Detroit*. With her husband, jazz guitarist-composer A. Spencer Barefield, she produces Palmer Woods Music in Homes, a series they started in 2007 showcasing jazz, classical, and world music in historic mansions and cool homes in Detroit's Palmer Woods neighborhood, which is located just north of Palmer Park. Barefield can be found with camera in one hand and her St. Bernard Devo in the other, promoting great jazz and music in Detroit, and helping to create events and happenings to revitalize Detroit.

**Sara Jane Boyers** is a California fine art photographer who, after successful careers in the music and publishing industries, has returned to a serious focus on her photography. In her work, Boyers searches for that iconic element of ordinary experience that defines the whole, choosing to render it subtly and with a sense of beauty that is provocative and demanding. Among her exhibition projects, *DETROIT:DEFINITION*, an ongoing study of her birth city as it again arises, has been exhibited at the Lillle3000/Renaissance Festival in Lille, France, and in Paris in fall 2016. A photograph from this project was on exhibition in Italy at the prestigious 2016 Venice Biennale/Architecture in the U.S. Pavilion, whose theme was Detroit, and again at MOCAD, Detroit in 2017.

**Michael Constantine McConnell** is originally from Detroit and is currently a proud resident of San Marcos, Texas, where he is pursuing a doctoral degree in Developmental Education at Texas State University and singing in degenerate Scots-Irish grunge-folk and Appalachian bluegrass/gothspel bands after sundown.

**Jill Day** is a writer, minister, and chronicler/historian who has a lifelong love for her birthplace, Detroit.

**Lakisha Dumas**, formerly Lakisha Jones, lived in the Detroit area most of her life. Born in 1977, Lakisha called the Mack and Conner area her home until her mother got married in 1986. She then moved not too far away to the Warren and Conner area on French Road where she lived until she moved to college at Eastern Michigan University. Lakisha went to Carlton Elementary, Damon J. Keith Elementary, Dorothy Fisher Middle School, and Laura F. Osborn High School. Detroit is a part of Lakisha and Lakisha will always be a part of Detroit because Detroit is in her heart and has made her the proud womAn she is today.

**Joel Fluent Greene** is a Detroit-based poet, author, and event curator. A Spirit Of Detroit Award winner, Joel was the long-running host of Detroit's iconic Cafe Mahogany poetry nights and has shared the stage with acts as diverse as The Roots, Pharrell, The Last Poets, Big Sean, Saul Williams, and the Detroit Red Wings. He has also acted as master of ceremonies at events for Chrysler Corporation, 100 Black Men of America, Inside-Out Detroit, and Music Hall Center. As former director of Music Hall Center's Words and Rhythms of the D outreach program, he has held workshops and performances in over fifty schools in the Metro Detroit area. Author of three collections of poetry—*WAXING/waning*, *Poems of Bungalow and Concrete*, and *Somewhere in the Middle: Love Poems*—Joel is currently producer and host of Mahogany @ The Museum, creative writing instructor at Mariner's Inn, and co-owner of Cass Corridor Card Company.

**Aaron Foley** is a writer who grew up in and currently lives in Detroit, which gives him more street cred than a lot of others. He has written for several local and national publications. His first book, *How to Live in Detroit Without Being a Jackass*, was published in 2015.

**R.J. Fox** is the award-winning writer of several short stories, plays, poems, and fifteen feature length screenplays. Two of his screenplays have been optioned to Hollywood. His most recent publication is a travel memoir entitled *Love and Vodka: My Surreal Adventures in Ukraine*, published through Fish Out of Water Books. His debut novel, *Awaiting Identification*, is set in Detroit and is scheduled to be released in fall 2017. His work has been published in over thirty literary magazines. Fox graduated from the University of Michigan with a BA in English and received a teaching certificate from Wayne State University. In addition to moonlighting as a writer, Fox teaches English and video production in the Ann Arbor Public Schools, where he uses his own dream to inspire his students to follow their own. He has also worked in public relations at Ford Motor Company and as a reporter. His website is www.foxplots. com. Or follow him on Twitter @foxwriter7.

**Cal Freeman** is the author of the book, *Brother of Leaving*, and the chapbook, *Heard Among the Windbreak*. He was born and raised in Warrendale, West Detroit. He currently lives in Dearborn, Michigan, and teaches at Oakland University.

**Julién Godman** is an Armenian American born in Detroit and raised on the road, following his mother's scholastic and slightly nomadic aspirations. Since moving back to Detroit in 2007, Julién has been actively involved in Detroit's social, civic, culinary, and artistic communities. Today, he works freelance for varied cultural events and in nonprofit grant writing, is known for his monthly health-based brunch popups, and runs his own herbal tea venture.

**Vince Guerrieri**, a regular Belt contributor, is a sportswriter who's gone straight. He saw Tommy Vardell (not Barry Sanders) score a touchdown at the Silverdome, sang along with the Lions fight song—to his wife's chagrin—watched a Stanley Cup Final game at Joe Louis Arena, and has been in the press box at Tiger Stadium and Comerica Park.

**Heather Harper** discovered the Parke-Davis buildings while working as a temporary moving assistant at the Skillman Foundation. A graduate of the Legal Assistant program at Macomb Community College, Heather enjoys learning about history and discovering new places. As an art lover and feature writer, her favorite things about Detroit are the various architectural styles and public artworks.

**Monica Hogan** grew up on Detroit's east side at the height of the baby-boom era with seven sisters and one brother. She studied creative writing at Wayne State University in Detroit, Hunter College in Manhattan, and the Writer's Center in Bethesda, Maryland. After more than two decades as a journalist, she lives near Washington, D.C., with her husband and daughter, but like millions of Detroit natives who remember the Motown-era with pride, she can't forget the Motor City.

**Elias Khalil** is a thirty-year resident of Detroit, sixteen of which have been in his Cass Corridor home. He is co-author of the 2012 book *Detroit's Cass Corridor*. Elias is a former educator of Economics, Politics, French, and Arabic. He has traveled extensively, both domestically and internationally, and has lived in France and

Senegal. Currently Elias is a small business entrepreneur and the co-owner of La Feria Spanish Tapas located in the Cass Corridor.

**Will T. Langford IV** is a poet, educator, and Fulbright Scholar who has worked extensively in East Africa. A graduate of Michigan State University, Will is the founder of the MSU Slam Poetry Team and a graduate of the Pennsylvania State University as well. Still, Detroit is where his heart is.

**Lhea J. Love** is a poet, novelist, and memoirist from Detroit, Michigan. She holds a degree in Philosophy and a minor in African and African American studies from the University of Michigan. Her fiction, nonfiction, and poetry have been published by the *Gettysburg Review*, *African American Review*, and *For Harriet*. In 2015, Lhea was selected as a Callaloo fellow for their annual writer's workshop. In 2016, Lhea's memoir was a Feminist Press debut book award finalist, judged by Tayari Jones. When Lhea is not reading or writing, she is either developing software or spending time with her six-year-old daughter, Harper Lee.

**Erin Marquis** is a lifelong metro-Detroiter who spent much of her childhood on the city's west side. While attending the University of Michigan-Dearborn, she started her journalism career covering everything from disgraced Mayor Kwame Kilpatrick's multiple court appearances to the spread of the emerald ash bore for 101.9 WDET. She is currently managing editor of the automotive news website *Jalopnik.com*. Erin lives in Detroit with her partner, dog, and several surviving tomato plants.

**Michelle Martinez** is a Latinx-Mestiza environmental justice activist, writer, and mother living and working in southwest Detroit. Since 2006, she has worked in local communities of color to build power to halt climate change and the detrimental effects of pollution in post-industrial Detroit. Working across issues of race, gender, and nationality, she has built and led coalitions using art and media, land-based programming, popular education, voter engagement, and corporate accountability tactics to shape policy solutions against environmental racism. Currently, she is the executive director of Third Horizon Consulting, which strives to empower people to make collective decisions strategically for more sustainable and equitable social change. She has a MS from the University of Michigan School of Nature Resources and Environment, and a BA in English Literature. She is an Equity Fellow at Wayne State University Law School's Damon J. Keith Center for Civil Rights. In her everyday life, she cares for her home and family as a gardener, mother, and artist.

**Maureen McDonald** is a veteran freelance writer who writes and blogs for *Crain's Detroit Business*, the *Hub of Detroit*, *Jewish News*, and a host of online publications. She ghostwrote a history book, *Sirens of Chrome: the Enduring Allure of Auto Show*, for Millennium Books; co-wrote *Royal Oak* for Arcadia Publishing; contributed to MyTown Miracles, a celebration of Detroit's leaders; and researched the hundredth anniversary of Henry Ford Health System. She has taught journalism and communications classes at Wayne State University, the University of Michigan–Dearborn and the University of Detroit Mercy. She serves on the board of the Michigan Journalism Hall of Fame. Maureen is an avid bicyclist who completed a ten-day bicycle tour of Ireland's south coast a few years back. She lived most of her life in Detroit and moved to Southfield to write a novel about growing up near the nation's first major shopping mall, Northland.

**Marsha Music**, daughter of a pre-Motown record producer, grew up in Highland Park and lives in the Lafayette Park community of Detroit. She is a self-described "Detroitist" and writes about the city's music and its past, present, and future. She is a former activist, labor leader, and a noted speaker. She has contributed to significant Detroit narratives, including *Untold Tales, Unsung Heroes: An Oral History of Detroit's African American Community*, 1918-1967, the University of Michigan's "Living Music Oral History Project;" *Thanks for the View, Mr. Mies: Lafayette Park, Detroit*; and *A Detroit Anthology*. She has appeared in documentary films such as HBO's *City on Fire: The 1968 Detroit Tigers*, and contributed narration in the movie *12th and Clairmount*. Marsha is an executive assistant in the judiciary, has two sons and four stepchildren, and is married to the artist David Philpot.

**Drew Philip**'s first book of nonfiction, *A $500 House in Detroit: Rebuilding an Abandoned Home and an American City*, is out from Scribner now and can be purchased wherever books are sold. He has bylines in the *Detroit Free Press*, *Buzzfeed*, and the *Guardian* among others, and lives in Detroit with his dog Gratiot in a house he built himself.

**Gail Rodwan** is a lawyer who has lived in Sherwood Forest with her photographer husband for the past forty-seven years. During that time, she has served on the board of directors of the Sherwood Forest Association in a variety of positions. She is the author of the 2017 book, *The Story of Sherwood Forest: One Hundred Years a Detroit Neighborhood*, which chronicles the history of one very special place.

**Justin Rogers** is a black poet, educator, coach, editor, and Best of the Net Nominee from the city of Detroit, Michigan. Rogers is an advocate for literacy among inner-city youth and the amplification of black voices. Performing around the Midwest and coordinating after-school, intensive creative-writing programming with InsideOut Literary Arts, Rogers actively shares poems surrounding living and growing as a black man in America. Rogers most recently has work published or forthcoming in *Tinderbox, Mobius Magazine, Apiary Magazine, 3Elements Review, Skip-Fiction, Gramma Press* and *Public Pool*. Rogers also is an editor with *Wusgood Magazine* and an adult adviser for the youth-led arts journal, *Underscore Review*.

**April S.C.**, a native Detroiter, by day runs a small business based in Southfield, Mich., and with her husband is working on brainwashing two small humans for the next decade and a half. Despite a short article on Inc.com for something totally unrelated, April can't say she is a writer yet, but would like to be one when she grows up.

**Bailey Sissoy Isgro** is the owner of Detroit History Tours and the Detroit History Club. She is an author, humorist, workaholic, and Faygo-loving tour guide from the great city of Detroit. She works as an automotive sculptor by day and by night she writes and lectures on the history of the American working woman, prostitution, and Detroit between the world wars. When she isn't tramping around Detroit giving tours, drinking at century-old bars, and talking history with anyone who'll join her, she can be found at her home in Highland Park. She is meticulous in her research and passionate about historical accuracy, yet she takes great joy in presenting history in the most exciting, playful, and accessible way possible; after all, owning a century-old brothel will increase anyone's sense of historical humor. A passionate connoisseur of all things delicious, she adamantly argues the health benefits of coney dogs and Vernors floats.

**Barbara Stewart Thomas** was born and raised in Detroit. Her family moved to Southfield before her senior year of high school, so she graduated from Southfield High rather than Mumford. She never did get the hang of suburban life. Stewart Thomas went to Michigan State University, but left before graduation to move to San Francisco. Then she moved to Dublin, Ireland, to be with the man whom she would eventually marry. He decided to go to Trinity College to major in Irish History. She got a chance to travel around Europe. She left before he did and reapplied to Michigan State where she finally earned her BA in 1974. Stewart Thomas moved to Dekalb, Illinois, in 1979 with her husband who ended up getting his PhD in Sociology and Criminology from Michigan State. He got a job on the faculty of Northern Illinois University. She worked at Northern Illinois in clerical jobs, but went back to school and got her MFA in Photography. She taught photography at Northern Illinois for twenty years. Stewart Thomas is retired and now lives in Chicago, back in the city again. She has been visiting Detroit a lot in the last few years, making photographs and taking great interest in everything that is going on there.

**Ian Thibodeau** is a Detroit-based writer and reporter who was raised in Dearborn, Michigan. He travels some, reads a lot, and occasionally writes letters to his fiancée, Josephine, on a loud, dusty electric Smith-Corona Coronet she bought him for Christmas a few years ago. Every now and then, he rolls by his dad's childhood home just so he doesn't forget. He lives on the city's northwest side in a two-bedroom flat dominated by twin tuxedo cats, Levi and Gouda.

**Lori Tucker-Sullivan** is a freelance writer whose poems, essays, stories, and reviews have appeared in various magazines and journals, including *Now and Then: The Magazine of Appalachia, Passages North*, the *Sun, About the Girl*, the *Cancer Poetry Project, Midwestern Gothic*, and others. Her essay, "Detroit, 2015," about her decision to return to Detroit after the death of her husband, was nominated for a Pushcart Prize and was listed as a Notable Essay of 2015 in *The Best American Essays 2016*. She is the author of the blog *A Widow's Apprenticeship*. She holds an MFA from Spalding University with a focus in Creative Nonfiction and is working on a memoir about how friendships with the widows of 1970's rock stars helped her on her grief journey.

**Zoë Villegas** is a writer and native Detroiter. She comes from a Mexican American family and has unparalleled love for the grit, glamour, and fringe of this city. From the hundreds of people she has met in line to pay bills, check out books, buy false eyelashes, pay for booze and potato chips, or wherever the tax for being poor may be paid that day, she never stops learning what Detroit is. She can always be found covered in glitter wherever the most raucous crowd is gathered that day.

**Jeff Waraniak** is a native metro-Detroiter turned Detroiter. He was a resident of Rivertown for three years while serving as an associate editor at *Hour Detroit* magazine, where he covered the city's people, food, history, sports, and more. His writing has also appeared in *Chicago Magazine, National Geographic* books, and *5280 Magazine* in Denver, Colorado.

**Scheherazade Washington Parrish** is a writer, educator, and muse from Detroit. She was writer-in-residence with InsideOut Literary Arts Program, as well as artist-in-residence with Spread Art, and currently teaches children that they are smart, and how, at the James & Grace Lee Boggs School.

**Hakeem Weatherspoon** graduated from Denby High School in 2014 and is studying journalism at Michigan State University. He also writes and performs poetry, and works to strengthen his neighborhood and others across the city.

# Acknowledgements

This anthology could not be possible without the continued support of Belt Publishing, whose mission in amplifying the voices of Detroit and her fellow Rust Belt cities is now much more critical than it ever has been. Thank you to Anne Trubek, Martha Bayne, and Nicole Boose for helping to bring this tome to light, and Haley Stone for—again!—delivering top-notch design work.

Thank you to the city of Detroit for making all of us contributors who we are, and for allowing us to represent you in ways only we could.